Yorkshire Dales

40 favourite walks

The author and publisher have made every effort to ensure that the information in this publication is accurate, and accept no responsibility whatsoever for any loss, injury or inconvenience experienced by any person or persons whilst using this book.

published by
pocket mountains ltd
The Old Church, Annanside, Moffat, DG10 9HB
pocketmountains.com

ISBN: 978-1-907025-54-9

Text and photography © Alastair Ross

The right of Alastair Ross to be identified as the Author of this work has been asserted by him in accordance with the Copyright, Designs and Patents Act 1988

A catalogue record for this book is available from the British Library

Contains Ordnance Survey data © Crown copyright and database right 2016, supported by out of copyright mapping 1945-1961

Printed in Poland

Introduction

The Dales gain their character from the geology which has formed them over millennia. Almost the whole area is built on Great Scar Limestone, most evident in the Craven Dales in the south. Here it is the limestone that forms the predominant landscape of well-drained grasslands, grazed by sheep, interspersed with white limestone scars and outcrops. Walking varies from delightful springy turf to complex limestone pavements and scars, with heather and rough moorland – more inclined to be squelchy underfoot – higher up. At the top of the pile is a cap of millstone grit, emerging only on the highest peaks.

Ingleborough, one of Yorkshire's 'Three Peaks', is arguably the most distinctive of the higher summits and it provides a vivid geological insight into the Dales. Its base is encircled by remarkable limestone karst, with some of the best examples of 'pavement' in the British Isles, protected as a National Nature Reserve. Above this, the mountainside rises steeply up a series of sandstone and shale terraces, overlaid by heather and peat, where the Yoredale Series rocks predominate. The very highest section is a hardy cap of millstone grit, evident in Ingleborough's iconic sloping plateau.

Being permeable, limestone has also allowed water to gouge out potholes and caves, leaving dry valleys above. These are common throughout the Craven Dales. At Malham, for example, water now flowing underground once thundered over the great wall at the Cove. Nearby, one of the most extensive cavern systems in Europe connects Gaping Gill with Ingleborough Cave. Just south of here, the Craven Faults mark the southern edge of the Dales, running almost parallel to the A65.

The Northern Dales are different in character. In Wensleydale and Swaledale, limestone is less evident, buried far below the surface, and shales and sandstones are more apparent. Where limestone is exposed it is of a different character. The long sinuous course of the Swale has carved a deep trench in the moorland, hiding woodland and small settlements, many originally Norse. It is here that the evidence of former lead mining is most readily seen in the haunting remains scattered across great swathes of moorland. These bear witness to the industrial importance and vitality of this area in the 18th and 19th centuries. Lead mining can be found elsewhere too, notably around Grassington, in Wharfedale and at Greenhow, above Nidderdale. Wensleydale has a very different terrain. Here the River Ure flows through more pastoral scenery, home to dairy farming and the eponymous Wensleydale cheese.

To the west, the rounded, convex Howgill Fells are reminiscent of the Southern Uplands in Scotland. Only the southern section was originally included in the National Park, with the small and historic town of Sedbergh sitting at the foot of the hills. The National Park's border excluded the northern uplands, which were located in the old county of Westmorland, running along the former county boundary and splicing the Howgills at their highest point, The Calf. In 2016, the Park was extended to include the northern section of the Howgills, as well as the limestone uplands around Orton and Kirkby Stephen. In total this covers well over 2000 sq km of land across the north of England.

The historic Dales
There is evidence of early settlement in the Yorkshire Dales, with examples of stone circles and early dwellings such as Attermire Cave near Settle. The Romans built forts, including one at Ilkley in Lower Wharfedale, and drove roads across the hills in order to join the settlements and defend their territory. Their road across Stainmore, north of the Dales, is still a key route across the Pennines used by the A66 from Scotch Corner as far as Penrith.

With the gradual disintegration of the Roman Empire, Angles, Danes and Vikings successively migrated into the area and the Anglo-Saxon Kingdoms of Deira and Northumbria emerged. The variety of place names indicates the eclectic origins of the people and traditions, with the Danish *by* and the Norse *thwaite* in common usage. The northern word 'force' derives from the Viking *foss* for 'waterfall'.

The Norman Conquest was hard on Yorkshire and it was subjugated savagely, though it was also subject to Scottish incursions from the north. But during this period monasteries also flourished and became an important foundation of trade and social care. Great communities such as Jervaulx Abbey were established. An extensive network of trade routes linked the Dales. Many of these survive as long-distance bridleways, such as the 'Langstrothdale Road' running north from Horton in Ribblesdale.

Lead mining thrived in the Dales, though the development of major industrial cities took place further south in Yorkshire. With the decline of the industry, many people moved away, but the long-standing wool trade and the expansion of dairy farming retained commerce and activity in even the remotest corners of the region. Tourism is now also a key economic earner.

Walking the Dales
This is superlative walking country. The floor of the Dales is carpeted by wildflowers in season. Above this, most of the region is open and unencumbered by fences or restrictions. The characteristic stone walls are ubiquitous. Many are centenarians and some are a lot older. There is little in the way of agricultural crops, except for grass, but bear in mind that hay is a very important product for farmers and treat meadows with suitable respect and care. In limestone country the ground is soft and well drained, mostly short cropped through grazing. The

higher areas offer fantastic views, in suitable weather!

There are a number of long-distance footpaths in the Dales. The most famous is the original one, the legendary Pennine Way, which runs through the length of the National Park from Gargrave in the south through Malham, Horton and Hawes to Keld, continuing beyond to the Scottish border. In contrast, the Dales Way is a gentler affair, heading from the conurbations of West Yorkshire to the Lake District via Wharfedale and Dentdale.

Alongside these long-distance paths is a plethora of formal and less formal routes, such as the 85km Nidderdale Way or the Ribble Way, following the river from source to sea. One of the best known challenge routes is the 39km Three Peaks, joining Ingleborough, Pen-y-ghent and Whernside and involving more than 1500m of climbing. Aside from the official routes, there are miles and miles of trails, tracks and packhorse routes. It is not difficult to design your own. Generally the paths and tracks are very well signposted and maintained.

Although the Dales are not as obviously rugged as some other mountainous areas in the north of Britain, the challenge that tackling this terrain entails should not be underestimated. Much of this country is quite remote with extensive high, rocky ground. Mist can occur at any time of year and winters are relatively hard, with snow a ready possibility in winter months and at other times. Becks and rivers can swell and flood, making fording them difficult. Appropriate clothing and footwear is essential, together with the use of a map and compass or GPS. The maps in this volume give a broad overview of the route you are to follow, but you should also use detailed maps such as the OS Explorer series or those produced by Harvey Maps.

Public transport

The remarkable Settle-Carlisle Railway bisects the Dales with a regular service between Leeds and Carlisle. All trains stop at Settle and Kirkby Stephen. Most also call at Horton in Ribblesdale, Ribblehead, Dent and Garsdale. Many of the walks start at or near these stations. Five trains a day run along the Bentham Line to Lancaster and Morecambe. For times visit northernrailway.co.uk.

Bus services can change, but several routes are key arteries. Most have regular services all week and all year, though varying in frequency.

A network of services is also organised by DalesBus on Sundays throughout the year and on Bank Holidays between Easter and August. These buses serve most areas of the Dales and routes start from West Yorkshire, East Lancashire, Teesside, York and Lancaster. Timetables and coverage vary between summer and winter. Details can be found at dalesbus.org.

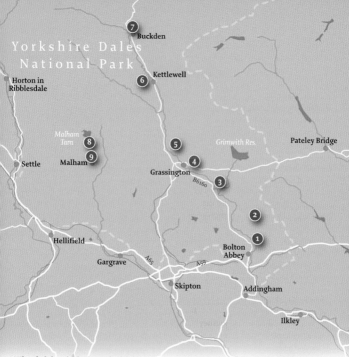

Wharfedale winds from the highest moorland of the Pennines through the limestone pastures of the Upper Dales. Historic settlements, such as Buckden, Kettlewell and Linton, were established along the banks of the River Wharfe and are now popular and picturesque visitor destinations. Other villages grew through industry, with Grassington being the centre for extensive lead mining. These haunting remains add to the evocative and wild atmosphere of the open moors.

Monastic, as well as industrial, Britain had many roots here, with photogenic reminders such as the ruins of Bolton Abbey framed by a loop in the river. Woodland is more evident in Wharfedale than in many of the other valleys and the river itself has a reputation for a fast and furious response to rainfall on the soggy moors that give rise to it.

A little way to the west, Malham has some of the best limestone scenery and features in the world. The precipitous cliff at Malham Cove and the dramatic formation of nearby Gordale Scar bear witness to the power of water and rock.

View over Kettlewell ▶

Wharfedale and Malhamdale

Bolton Abbey and the River Wharfe

Distance 11km (or 3km shorter loop)
Time 3 hours (or 1 hour shorter loop)
Terrain riverside and woodland paths
Map OS Explorer OL2 **Access** buses from
Ilkley and Grassington and Sunday
DalesBus from Ilkley and Leeds to
Bolton Abbey village

Bolton Abbey is a popular destination
for day visitors from West Yorkshire and
the surrounding area. The ruins of the
12th-century Augustinian Priory, closed
in 1539 as part of Henry VIII's Dissolution
of the Monasteries, lie in a loop in the
River Wharfe. The abbey has given its
name to the attractive village and
to the Duke of Devonshire's Yorkshire
seat. The grounds are still owned and
managed by the estate.

Leaving the car park in Bolton Abbey,
turn left onto the B6160 to follow this for
a short way to the village green. On the
right-hand side of the road, go through
the gap in the wall just to the left of the
Tea Cottage. On the far side, a gate opens
out to a magnificent panorama of the
abbey ruins with the River Wharfe beyond.
Follow the path down towards the river,
walking through an area that was once
used by medieval monks for fish ponds.
Cross the river on the bridge. Bear left on
the far side, following the rising path
through woodland and away from the
riverbank. A well-engineered route climbs
along the top of the bank through beech
woodland, with fantastic views across the
river and around the abbey ruins. Descend
to a road and follow it left.

A footbridge avoids the ford; on the far
side, leave the road to continue on the
riverside path to the left. This cuts a level

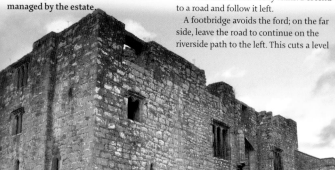

course across waterside meadows to reach a wooden bridge opposite Cavendish Pavilion. (For a shortcut, you can cross the bridge to the Pavilion, which includes a café and extensive gift shop.)

To reach Barden Bridge, do not cross but carry on along the riverside path, passing through woodland and briefly joining the road before continuing on a permissive waterside route for another 3.5km. Reach the road and cross the Wharfe on Barden Bridge. On the far side, turn left along a permissive path to follow the opposite bank downstream. The path goes through the Strid, where the river has forced a narrow cutting through the rock and descends a sequence of rapids. In just under 4km reach Cavendish Pavilion.

From here, follow the riverbank south, through the parking area. At the end of this, take the path heading uphill towards the Cavendish Memorial on the skyline. The elaborate drinking fountain honours Lord Frederick Cavendish who was murdered in Dublin's Phoenix Park in 1882 on his first day of duty as Chief Secretary for Ireland. His assassins were members of the Irish National Invincibles, a radical splinter group of the Irish Republican Brotherhood, a secret oath-bound organisation dedicated to Irish independence from the United Kingdom. It is an excellent viewpoint over the loop in the river and the abbey.

Continue alongside the road for about 250m, before bearing left along a driveway towards the priory. Pass the ruin, part of which is still used as the parish church. Keep ahead on the driveway to return to the road and Bolton Abbey village.

Simon's Seat and the Valley of Desolation

Distance 11km **Time** 4 hours
Terrain woodland track leads to exposed
moorland paths **Map** OS Explorer OL2
Access buses from Ilkley and Grassington
and Sunday DalesBus from Ilkley and
Leeds to Bolton Abbey village, 2km from
the start

Simon's Seat is a craggy outcrop presiding
over Mid Wharfedale at a height of 485m.
There are at least two accounts as to how
it got its name: one that it is named after
a child once found here by a shepherd and
given the name Simon; another that this
was a site of Druid worship named after
the legendary Simon Magus. Either way,
the top is a remote and atmospheric spot,
as well as a splendid viewpoint. Climbing
from the picturesque valley at Bolton
Abbey, this route passes through the
Valley of Desolation which is far from
desolate but owes its name to a huge
storm and deluge in 1826.

Start at the car park at Cavendish
Pavilion (charge), where there is a gift
shop and café. Note that this walk is
across land covered by an access
agreement that predates the CROW Act.
No dogs are allowed and the route may
occasionally be closed for shooting.

From Cavendish Pavilion, cross the
River Wharfe on the wooden bridge, then
turn left along the riverside footpath,
following the signpost. After about 300m,
leave the riverside and climb up to the
road (SP Simon's Seat). Turn left and
continue climbing along the lane for
about 300m before turning right through
a gate by Waterfall Cottage (SP Simon's
Seat). From here, the walk is over access
land on a permissive path and no dogs are
permitted. The conquest of Simon's Seat
begins with a gradual ascent through
parkland, rising out of the Wharfe Valley
and alongside the wooded cleft of
Posforth Gill. Pass a little pond on the

◄ Simon's Seat

right; a small footpath leads left down into the gill to view the waterfall. The main track keeps ahead, soon becoming a narrower path, winding up above the waterfalls deep in the ravine below. Cross a footbridge into the Valley of Desolation. A narrow path goes through the ravine, over rocks and tree roots. It resumes the ascent through oak trees to reach a gate.

Beyond this, the path rises through a plantation. Keep straight ahead at a junction, now on a good woodland track. At the top of the hill, the plantation ends at a gate. Ahead lies the open fellside. An excellent landrover track soon crosses the ford at Great Agill Bottom and climbs steadily through the heather moorlands of Barden Fell. It sweeps left around the head of Great Agill Beck and then back to the right. After nearly 2km of moorland, come to a rough T-junction. The main track seems to go left, but the route to the summit lies along the lesser path veering right. The path is rough, rocky and wet in places, but is clear enough as it heads towards the ragged tor on the skyline. It wanders through the wilderness of loose gritstone and heather, winding up to the summit of Simon's Seat.

The summit is at the head of a steep scarp, dropping away to Skyreholme far below, and the northern side of Simon's Seat is very different from the route you have climbed. From the vantage point by the OS column, you have a bird's eye view across the valley of Skyreholme Beck and Trollers Gill, with the wild moors between the Wharfe and the Nidd stretching to the blue horizon. Return by the outward route, following the path back to Waterfall Cottage and on to Cavendish Pavilion.

Map labels:

Simon's Seat
Lord's Seat
Barden Fell
Lower Fell Plantation
Carncliff Top
Great Agill Bottom
Laund Pasture Plantation
Valley of Desolation
River Wharfe
Posforth Gill
To Grassington
B6160
Cavendish Pavilion
Bolton Park Farm
To Bolton Abbey

0   1km

Trollers Gill

Distance 12km **Time** 4 hours
Terrain riverside paths and limestone
tracks **Map** OS Explorer OL2
Access buses from Ilkley and Grassington
and Sunday DalesBus from Ilkley and
Leeds to Burnsall

According to legend, the limestone gorge
of Trollers Gill is the home of Barghest, a
mythical hound that may even have part-
inspired Arthur Conan Doyle's *The Hound
of the Baskervilles*. Fables aside, the deep
ravine is impressive – for much of the
year the headwaters of Skyreholme Beck
are absorbed by the porous rock, but in
spate a torrent of water cascades down
the narrow canyon. The outward journey
follows a footpath alongside the River
Wharfe, concluding with a glorious high-
level stroll back to Burnsall.

Start from the National Park car park
near Burnsall Bridge. There is also some
roadside parking available in the village,
which offers a range of cafés and pubs.

The first part of the walk follows the
Dales Way downstream. Cross the Wharfe
on Burnsall Bridge and follow the road for
another 100m. Turn right, taking a
footpath across a field and then above the
left bank of the river. A pleasant path
follows the river for 3.5km to Howgill,
either through meadows or along the
wooded slopes above the river. Ash trees
line the water's edge.

On reaching a road at Howgill, leave the
Dales Way to turn left. After 200m along
the lane, cross a stile on the right and
follow the path (SP Skyreholme). You
have now turned up a side valley of the
Wharfe and a grass path undulates across
a series of fields above Fir Beck. The right
of way goes above a caravan site and finds
a track. This leads past Howarth Farm to a
lane. Turn right and walk through the
hamlet of Skyreholme, overshadowed by
Simon's Seat, the steep edge crowned by
a rocky tor 485m above sea level.

In 700m, at a road junction next to an

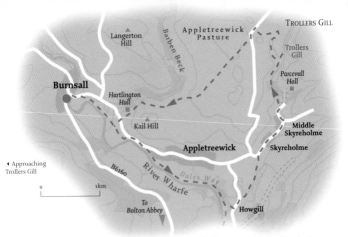

Langerton
Hill

Appletreewick
Pasture

Barben Beck

Trollers
Gill

Parcevall
Hall

Burnsall

Hartlington
Hall

Kail Hill

Middle
Skyreholme

Appletreewick

Skyreholme

◄ Approaching
Trollers Gill

B6160

River Wharfe

Dales Way

0   1km

To
Bolton Abbey

Howgill

old red phonebox, turn left (SP Parcevall Hall). Follow this no-through road for about 300m. Just before a wooden bridge over Skyreholme Beck, turn left through a gate (SP New Road). Across the beck is historic Parcevall Hall, now used as a church conference centre. The extensive and varied gardens were laid out from 1927 and are open to view the public. Follow the path alongside Skyreholme Beck, rising into the steep-sided valley, studded with limestone boulders and scree. In just under 1km after leaving the road, the path forks. The route you are following bears left up a dry valley but, first, continue straight ahead to view the hidden gorge of Trollers Gill. As the path rounds the corner the ravine is revealed; in spate the force makes a dramatic sight; on most occasions the limestone will swallow the water to a hidden underground passage.

Returning to the path junction, follow a lovely, firm grass path up the dry valley, climbing out of the dale. It becomes a track, winding past a disused lead mine and up on to the moor. Watch out for a yellow waymark post on the left which marks the point where the public footpath leaves the track and squelches across the moor to reach a road. (Nothing will be lost if you miss this and stay on the track which also reaches the same road.)

Turn left, following the road around a left-hand bend. In another 200m, turn right through a gate, taking a bridleway (SP Hartlington). A good level track offers panoramic views across Wharfedale and beyond. It then descends gradually to reach farm buildings about 2km from the road. Pass to the right of these and continue steadily downhill on the track, with the impressive pile of Hartlington Hall looming out of the trees across the deep defile of Barben Beck. At the bottom, cross the road and continue on the bridleway opposite. In 200m, reach the river and the Dales Way. Turn right and follow your outward steps to Burnsall.

13

Hebden Ghyll and Grassington Moor

Distance 11km **Time** 3 hours 30
Terrain riverside path, stony tracks and
quiet lanes **Map** OS Explorer OL2
Access buses from Skipton and Ilkley and
Sunday DalesBus from Leeds and Burnley
to Grassington

**Water, limestone and lead all contribute
to the unique landscape of Upper
Wharfedale. This walk follows the Dales
Way beside the River Wharfe before
passing through Hebden village into the
rocky recess of Hebden Ghyll. Above, on
the wilderness of Grassington Moor, are
the evocative remains of lead mines. The
old lead workings can be dangerous, so be
careful if you explore away from the path.**

There is a large car park (charge) at the
National Park Centre in Grassington. At
the far end of the overspill area, a paved
footpath leads to Linton Falls, dropping
downhill to the Wharfe and arriving at a
footbridge. You can observe the falls from
here; when the river is in spate water
foams and tumbles over the rocky ledges,
leaving no doubt about its power.

Just short of the bridge, turn left across
a stile and take the path alongside the
river (SP Hebden, Burnsall). This is the
Dales Way which links West Yorkshire to
the Lake District. The ancient settlement
of Linton lies on the far bank, with the
parish church at the end of the village.
Cross a couple of fields, follow a lane past
a fish farm and then carry on along
riverside meadows. Notice the challenging
stepping stones across the river (for
another time) as you continue along the
Dales Way on an excellent gravelled path.

As the valley narrows, the banks close in
with horse chestnut, sycamore and ash
trees trailing down to the water's edge.
About 3km from Linton Falls you come to
a graceful suspension bridge across the
river. You could stay on the Dales Way as
it crosses here and then continue along
the opposite bank to the picturesque
riverside honeypot of Burnsall, where
there is an infrequent bus service back to
Grassington. But this walk leaves the river
here and turns left along a signed path for
Hebden. After 100m, join a lane, turn right

◀ Linton Falls

and, in another 100m, just beyond a bridge, turn left (SP Hebden and Bank Head). Pass a few houses and gardens, entering a wood by a kissing gate to shadow a small beck along a narrow limestone valley, before climbing to a lane. Go through another kissing gate and turn right along the lane into Hebden village, where you will find a shop, tearoom and pub.

Cross Hebden's main road and take the small road opposite. Leaving the village behind, begin the gentle ascent into the upper dale. The scenery changes as the beck carves a deep trench between bracken-clad slopes strafed with rocky outcrops. The road ends at a collection of houses at Hole Bottom. Keep straight ahead, past a row of cottages onto a bridleway beyond, signed for Yarnbury.

The wide track crosses the beck and then climbs along the opposite bank in wild open country. The valley, now known as Hebden Ghyll, marks the boundary between permeable limestone and coarse gritstone which is the characteristic geological profile of much of the Dales.

You are also now entering lead mining country and, further up, the remains of old structures and spoil heaps come into view as the bridleway becomes rougher,

fords the beck and continues along a better track on the far side. Continue to climb through the old workings, with the beck much diminished by the voracious appetite of the porous limestone.

The mines on Grassington Moor had their heyday in the mid-19th century when they produced almost 1000 tons of lead a year and employed up to 170 people. The track winds left up out of the valley and then passes through a gate to the vast lunar landscape at the top of the moor; a small clump of trees on the horizon indicates the location of Yarnbury and the Duke's New Road, a wide mining track which leads to it. At Yarnbury, go left to follow the very quiet lane for 3km to Grassington, with expansive views as far as the whaleback profile of Pendle Hill and the hills of Wharfedale.

15

Conistone Dib and Grass Wood

Distance 12km **Time** 4 hours
Terrain limestone uplands and woodland
paths; one short (avoidable) scramble
Map OS Explorer OL2 **Access** buses from
Skipton and Ilkley and Sunday DalesBus
from Leeds and Burnley to Grassington

A fantastic circuit of the uplands north of
Grassington. The limestone country is a
joy to walk, with soft springy turf and
broad horizons leading to the dramatic
dry valley of Conistone Dib. The return
weaves through some of the most
ancient woodland in the Dales,
conserved as a nature reserve.

If you're driving, the easiest place to
park in Grassington is the large car park at
the National Park Centre (charge). From
here walk to the marketplace, the
attractive square at the heart of the
village. Take the left of the two roads
rising from the far end of the marketplace.
In 200m come to another small square
and turn left along Chapel Street
(SP Dales Way). Pass the Methodist chapel
and, in 300m, turn right at Bank Lane
(SP Dales Way). The lane almost

immediately bends to the left and
becomes a track, leaving the town. In
another 200m, by a farmyard, come to a
junction of tracks. Leave the track here to
pass through a gate onto a field path
(easily missed).

The well-trodden route of the Dales Way
meanders through the classic upland
pattern of small stone-walled fields. Signs,
markers and stiles guide you. The route
passes through the site of a medieval
village, perched on a shelf just above the
floor of the dale. On a murky day the
spatters of limestone blend in with the
grey sky, but on a bright day the same
rocks seem illuminated by the sunlight.
Continue on the Dales Way, ignoring any
side turnings. At the top of a small rise
there's a restored lime kiln on the left,
dating from the mid-19th century. About
400m beyond this, you come to a path
crossing next to a wall.

To avoid the short scramble at the top

of Conistone Dib, you can bear left here, leaving the Dales Way, following a sign to Conistone and heading towards a mast. This path leads down a small dry valley to reach Conistone Dib in about 400m. Otherwise, carry straight on along the Dales Way. About 400m further on, come to the head of a cleft in the limestone, known as Conistone Dib. Just before the wall, find a footpath through a gate, leading down into the cleft. An initial easy scramble leads to a stony path down into the dry valley. Towards the bottom of the Dib, the broad grassy valley narrows into a funnel and a dramatic gorge winds through steep rocks guarded by ash trees. You emerge abruptly in the tiny village of Conistone.

There is a road junction in the centre of the village. Turn left and follow the road towards Grassington for 200m, passing a hostel and chapel on the left. Then go left onto a footpath at the side of a building (SP Grassington). A delightful track angles gently across the hillside, with a carpet of wildflowers in season. After about 1km, it curves left and winds around the deep wooded trench of Dib Beck. Across the gulf, ash trees cling to great limestone buttresses. At the head of the valley the path veers right and climbs the other side. You soon reach a junction next to a gate.

Don't go left through this. Instead follow the path as it bears right and enters a wonderful area of limestone heathland, studded with silver birch trees and carpeted with wildflowers. At a wall, cross the stile into Grass Wood Nature Reserve. The path weaves through the trees for another 300m to reach a path junction. Turn left onto a broad path leading to Grassington. This descends through the shady recesses of the ancient Grass Wood, with ferns, lichens and moss. Pass the site of a prehistoric settlement, before crossing a stile and leaving the wood. The path now crosses a couple of fields before reaching Cove Lane, leading back into Grassington.

◀ Above Grassington

17

Kettlewell, Littondale and Knipe Scar

Distance 10km Time 3 hours
Terrain steep rocky paths and level
riverside meadows Map OS Explorer OL30
Access buses from Skipton and Sunday
DalesBus from Leeds to Kettlewell

Although modest in distance this walk
explores three distinctive Dales
landscapes: well-drained limestone
pasture, heather moor and riverside
floodplain. It tackles some steep climbs,
with rocky sections, though navigation is
unlikely to be a problem and there are
some fantastic views.

Kettlewell is a charming limestone
village straddling Wharfedale between the
lofty heights of Great Whernside and the
steep ridge that separates Wharfedale and
its satellite, Littondale. It buzzes with
activity for much of the time. Although
many of its houses are holiday homes, it
is served by no fewer than three pubs, an
excellent village store and several
teashops. There is a small car park
provided by the National Park and other

alternative offerings (all chargeable),
but limited roadside parking.

Cross the river by Kettlewell Bridge. On
the far side, there are two footpaths to the
right. Take the left-hand one of these
(SP Arncliffe). A short way after the gate,
bear left, leaving the main track for a
footpath up the valley side (SP Arncliffe).
This rises inexorably, steepening as it
approaches a stone scar on the hillside.
The reward is an expansive view back
across the dale and beyond to Great
Whernside, looming above Kettlewell.
The scar is tackled by a steep but
straightforward stony gully. You will
probably need to use your hands, but
there is no technical difficulty and it is
not exposed. Beyond, the path continues
its ascent to arrive at the wall on the crest
of the ridge.

From here, enjoy extensive views of the
classic U-shaped, glaciated valley of the
Wharfe. Cross the stile, and then a second
one, to begin the descent towards
Littondale. The dry, springy turf of

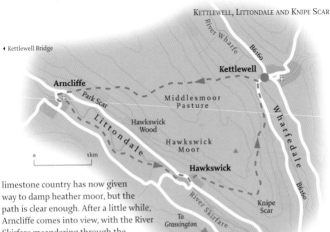

◄ Kettlewell Bridge

limestone country has now given way to damp heather moor, but the path is clear enough. After a little while, Arncliffe comes into view, with the River Skirfare meandering through the meadows on the floodplain. Towards the bottom, the moor gives way to woodland. A gate leads through a wall and immediately on to the top of Park Scar.

Negotiate the route down this steep rocky section with care, continuing on a path through the woods below. A final field leads to a lane. Go straight across the road and follow a footpath alongside the river, with the church opposite. At the end turn left to cross the Skirfare by the roadbridge. It is worth pausing to explore the dalehead settlement of Arncliffe. Most of the village is built around a large green, sporting its own pub at the far end.

Almost immediately after the bridge, bear left along a driveway, in front of the entrance to the church. The footpath goes between two houses and then continues alongside or near the river for the next 3km. On the approach to Hawkswick, you come to a footbridge. Cross the river here, then turn right to walk through the

village. Where the road bends right, turn left to take the track signed to Kettlewell.

This soon leaves the village and the path ascends steadily for over 1km. When you have nearly reached the top, look out for a path junction, marked by a small cairn. Turn left here, now climbing a short distance to reach a stile on the crest of the ridge. Cross this and continue towards Wharfedale which lies in front of you. There are apparently two paths, but either will do. After maintaining height, descend in earnest. In about 1km, you arrive at an opening in the wall, next to a stile just above a conifer wood. Continue into the wood, winding downhill through conifers and coppiced woodland. Eventually, you meet the road a little way short of Kettlewell. To avoid this last section of road walking, you can take the permissive path which runs more or less parallel to the road and back to Kettlewell.

The Head of Wharfedale

Distance 9km **Time** 3 hours **Terrain** tracks and hillside paths, with riverside return; some beck crossings may be difficult in very wet weather **Map** OS Explorer OL30 **Access** buses from Skipton and Sunday DalesBus from Leeds to Buckden

A circular walk, contouring around the head of Wharfedale and enjoying a magnificent panorama. Wharfedale turns west here and becomes known as Langstrothdale, rising to the Pennine watershed a few miles away. Cray Gill has gouged a course from the limestone slopes of Buckden Pike and joins the main valley near Hubberholme. No less than three pubs offer refreshments along the way, at Buckden, Cray and Hubberholme.

Buckden itself was established by the Norman rulers as the centre of a royal hunting forest. It still has an 'end of the road' feel, lying in a broad amphitheatre at the head of Wharfedale. It lies close to the watershed between the Southern and Northern Dales at Kidstones Pass and the

east-west spine of northern England. Start from the National Park car park (charge), though there is also some roadside parking. At the far end of the car park, go through the gate into the National Trust's Upper Wharfedale Estate. Buckden Rake is a good stone track that slants up the hillside for 1km, hazel and sycamore trees clinging to the steep slopes and limestone scree. As you gain height, enjoy the panoramic views across the amphitheatre at the head of the dale. In 1km, go through the gate onto open hillside. Kidstones Pass lies ahead on the horizon, carrying the road from Wharfedale over the watershed into Bishopdale. At the point where the main track levels off, it bends to the right heading directly for the summit of Buckden Pike. Ignore this and keep straight ahead on the level grass track through a gate (SP Cray High Bridge). Waterfalls sparkle in the distance.

Continue along a grassy terrace until you are just above the hamlet of Cray. To reach the settlement directly, you could cut down the hillside by taking a footpath

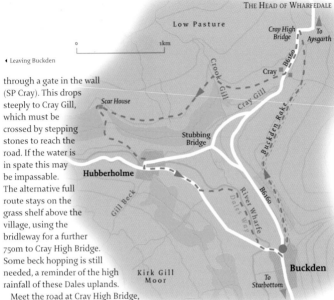

THE HEAD OF WHARFEDALE

Low Pasture

Cray High Bridge

To Aysgarth

Crook Gill

Cray

B6160

Scar House

Cray Gill

Buckden Rake

Stubbing Bridge

Hubberholme

Gill Beck

River Wharfe

Dales Way

B6160

Kirk Gill Moor

Buckden

To Starbottom

◄ Leaving Buckden

through a gate in the wall (SP Cray). This drops steeply to Cray Gill, which must be crossed by stepping stones to reach the road. If the water is in spate this may be impassable. The alternative full route stays on the grass shelf above the village, using the bridleway for a further 750m to Cray High Bridge. Some beck hopping is still needed, a reminder of the high rainfall of these Dales uplands.

Meet the road at Cray High Bridge, just a short way from the top of Kidstones Pass. Turn left and cross the bridge. Look out for the waterfall just off the road to the right. Follow the road for 750m until you arrive at Cray – there are just a few buildings here, but one of them is a pub! Follow the track at the back of the White Lion Inn (SP Stubbing Bridge & Yockenthwaite). The path continues above the farm buildings and along a grassy terrace, overlooking the sharp nick in the hillside cut by Cray Gill. Veer right to cross Crook Gill by a footbridge. Continue along the top of a limestone scar, soon with excellent views across the classic glacial U-shaped valley of Wharfedale.

Some 2.5km after Cray, you come to a junction just above the buildings at Scar House. At the fingerpost, turn left (SP Hubberholme). Pass the house and follow the access drive, descending into the valley to reach the small hamlet of Hubberholme. Pass the picturesque Norman church and cross the river. The George, on the opposite bank, is the last pub in the dale, and it keeps a candle on the bar to indicate it is open and in business. Facing the pub, turn left and follow the lane for about 700m. At a sign for Buckden Bridge, take the footpath through fields and beside the river to regain the road by the bridge. Go left to arrive in Buckden.

Malham Tarn

Distance 6km **Time** 1 hour 30
Terrain fairly level with tracks, lanes
and small paths **Map** OS Explorer OL2
Access Sunday DalesBus from Malham
and Settle to Malham Tarn (summer only)

Malham Tarn is the largest natural lake
in the Dales. Its shallow waters and
surrounding wetland form a National
Nature Reserve, providing habitats
for a rich variety of birdlife such as
lapwing, curlew, snipe, redshank and
oystercatcher. Its location at 330m above
sea level, with a backdrop of limestone
and woodland, gives this isolated sheet
of water a haunting tranquillity. This
easy walk encircles the tarn, though the
return crosses peaty moorland. However,
you can choose to extend the walk by
starting from Malham village (as
described at the end of this route).

Start from the National Trust car park
on the moorland road near the tarn. From
the end of the car park, follow the
Pennine Way sign on a grassy path

heading towards the tarn. Ahead lies a
wide plateau encircled by limestone scars
and, in the distance, the peak of
Fountains Fell. In the foreground, the
shimmering waters are backed by the
woodland around the idyllic setting of
Malham Tarn House. Passing east of the
tarn, the path curves slightly to the right,
skirting to the right of a walled copse. Go
through a gate to join a track which
continues as a shallow causeway through
a marshy area before drawing alongside
the tarn. A cattle grid takes the track into
the woods, climbing away from the shore
towards Malham Tarn House. This was
originally built as a shooting lodge, but
has been a field studies centre since 1948.

In 1858, Charles Kingsley visited the
house and thereafter chose the Dales as
the setting for his novel *The Water Babies*.

Stay on the track going past the back of
the house and descend as it becomes an
access road with views across the water
through the trees. Approaching some
cottages, stay on the lane as the Pennine

Way turns off to the right. About 200m after Shepherd's Cottage, turn left, leaving the road to follow a permissive bridleway. A level track continues just around the fringe of the marshes. This wetland makes up part of the National Nature Reserve and is host to many species, including willows, rushes and rare sedges and mosses.

A boardwalk is provided if you want to deviate from the track and explore the fen. The track ends at a gate. Join a road here and keep straight ahead. In 300m, bear left at the road junction, climbing slightly towards and beyond the buildings at High Trenhouse. After 800m, you come to a crossroads.

If you are short of time you can turn left and follow the road back to the car park. Otherwise, cross a stile with a marker post, just to the left of the road ahead. Aim for the remains of an old smelting chimney in the distance. A faint path traces the route across rough pasture, though in clear weather the goal is obvious. On reaching the restored chimney, keep straight ahead on a vague path, ignoring the waymark pointing left. Trend gently uphill, aiming for another post in the distance. Keep heading uphill past other intermittent posts to arrive at a

wall corner. Follow the wall for a short way and then cross a stile, just above an old barn. Continue along the opposite side, passing some scattered limestone clints, before dropping to a gap in a wall. Join a bridleway here and follow it back to the car park.

To start the route in Malham village, use the Pennine Way as a link between the village and the tarn in both directions. This more than doubles the walk distance to 13km. Begin by walking to Malham Cove (see p24). From there, continue on the Pennine Way along Watlowes Dry Valley in spectacular limestone scenery, reaching the tarn car park near Water Sinks, where the outflow from the tarn normally disappears into the thirsty limestone bedrock.

Malham Cove and Gordale Scar

Distance 6km **Time** 2 hours
Terrain stone and grass paths with a
steep ascent; some careful footwork
needed **Map** OS Explorer OL2
Access buses from Skipton and Sunday
DalesBus from Leeds and York to Malham

The village of Malham lies close to a
series of faultlines marking the
boundary between the limestone
uplands of the Dales and the lower-lying
pass through the northern hills, known
as the Aire Gap. This geology has created
a sequence of remarkable limestone
features, notably Malham Cove and
nearby Gordale Scar, cradling the village
and the upper dale and signalling the
start of rare and precious karst scenery.
The modest distance of this expedition
belies the unique and impressive rock
scenery you encounter.

Malham is reached by a road leaving the
A65 at Gargrave. There is a car park
(charge) at the National Park Centre at the
southern end of Malham; some roadside
parking is also available. From the
National Park Centre, walk up through the
village, past the Buck Inn, and keep
straight ahead. At the end of the village,
just past Town Head, turn right through a
gate. Walk along the well-surfaced
footpath to Malham Cove, the great
limestone cliff looming ahead. This
popular stone path is the Pennine Way
and passes through meadows of
buttercups and thistles, with ash trees
bordering the beck to the right. Spend a
few minutes at the base of the crag,
marvelling at the massive wall ahead.

The Cove is a favourite destination for
geography classes from Yorkshire and
Lancashire, a dramatic exposition of the
region's topography and history. The 75m-
high cliff was once a mighty waterfall
with the headwaters of the Aire, spawned
by the marshy surroundings of Malham
Tarn, crashing over the lip of the Cove.
Now they seep underground and emerge

24

◀ Malham Cove

lower down Malhamdale on the way to the Humber Estuary. Just before reaching the cliff, bear left to follow the footpath which climbs the left-hand side of the precipice using a sequence of steps.

At the top, turn right and cross the limestone pavement with great care. The stone can be slippery, especially when damp. The blocks of limestone (clints) have been weathered to form deep fissures (grikes). Herb-Robert, spleenwort and hart's tongue fern grow in these sheltered crannies.

There are expansive views southwards across the Aire Gap towards Pendle Hill and the South Pennines. At the far side of the pavement, the Pennine Way turns left towards Malham Tarn. To stay on this walk, go through the gate and follow the path bearing right (SP Gordale). In less than 1km, cross a road and continue through a gate on the opposite side.

The path leads downhill, with a wall on the right, and later drops more steeply down a couple of fields to reach the road at Gordale Bridge. A convenient refreshment van is often here. Turn left and follow the road for 200m, before taking a footpath to the left (SP Gordale Scar). This broad stony track follows the beck, passing through a campsite. It turns right into a dramatic enclosed amphitheatre at Gordale Scar, the

remains of a cave that collapsed many centuries ago. A waterfall spurts through the gap, enclosed by the high stone walls on either side.

Return to Gordale Bridge and follow the road beyond for a further 200m. Turn left onto a footpath (SP Riverside, Malham). The gravel path drops through shady woodland and an enchanting sylvan cascade at Janet's Foss. It continues through a rocky gorge, shaded by sycamore and ash trees, with occasional limestone outcrops towering above the path. The woods give way to a meadow path following the river. As it meets the Pennine Way, turn right for a short hop on the long-distance path into Malham.

25

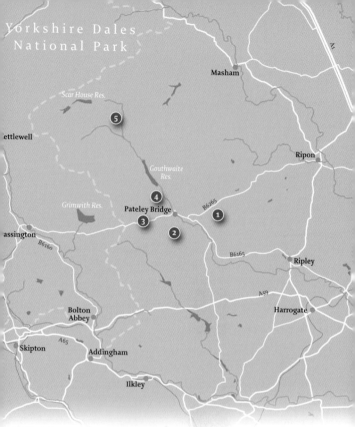

Nidderdale is not part of the National Park, but very much belongs to the Yorkshire Dales. The area is protected as an Area of Outstanding Natural Beauty, focused around the busy and popular centre of Pateley Bridge. Water is a theme here: it's collected in the mighty reservoirs at the head of the dale,

disappears through limestone crevices in the riverbed and has sculpted the great ravine at How Stean Gorge and the weird rock formations at Brimham. Generally, the floor of the dale is wooded and pastoral, while the slopes rise to open moorland with wide skies across the spine of northern England.

Nidderdale

Brimham Rocks and Fell Beck

Distance 6.5km **Time** 2 hours
Terrain paths and bridleways, including
some narrow riverside sections
Map OS Explorer 298 **Access** Sunday
DalesBus from Harrogate to Brimham
Rocks (summer only)

Water has eroded the millstone grit to
form the bizarre rock formations at
Brimham. Many of the natural sculptures
have names, such as the Dancing Bear,
the Smartie Tube, the Idol and the
Sphinx, though you may need some
imagination to interpret these titles!
After wandering through the rocks,
the walk descends to the woodland
valley and rocky ravine of Fell Beck, then
climbs back through the charming
hamlet of Smelthouses.

Start at the National Trust car park
(charge) on Brimham Moor Road, 3km
from the B6165 at Summerbridge. From

the car park, walk north through the
Rocks towards the visitor centre. You can
use the main vehicle track, but preferably
take the narrower path to the left,
meandering among the weird rock
formations. Both routes arrive in front of
the visitor centre. Now take the track
passing to the left of the centre, twisting
through woodland and between the
natural rock sculptures. It leads quite near
a cliff edge, so take care.

At the end of the cliff, drop slightly to a
dip in the ground, following the path as it
goes down the groove to the left and
ignoring the options that continue ahead
onto open moorland. In about 400m the
path meets a broad track by a National
Trust boundary marker. Turn sharp left
and walk along the track for 350m. When
it curves right into High North Pasture
Farm, carry straight on along the public
footpath that skirts the edge of the farm

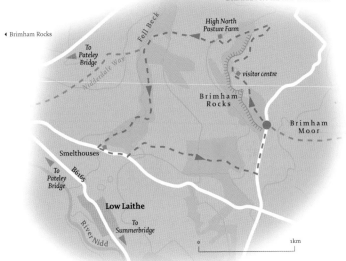

◀ Brimham Rocks

To Pateley Bridge

Fell Beck

High North Pasture Farm

Nidderdale Way

visitor centre

Brimham Rocks

Brimham Moor

Smelthouses

B6165

To Pateley Bridge

Low Laithe

To Summerbridge

River Nidd

0   1km

and garden. Briefly join another track on the far side before it, too, bends to the right around the garden. At this point, keep straight ahead to cross a stile and continue on the field footpath. Follow the right of way down several fields, with waymarks confirming the route. Reaching the bottom of the valley, you come to Fell Beck next to a ford and footbridge.

Staying on the same bank, turn left to take a woodland path which rises slightly above the beck. In a short while, keep roughly straight ahead at a staggered junction (SP Smelthouses). A clear path wanders through pleasant silver birch woodland. After about 600m, it makes a U-turn to the right, just in front of some ruined brick buildings, and then drops to the beck beside another footbridge. This

time, cross the water and continue downstream on the opposite bank. The narrow path clings to the riverbank above a steep ravine while the beck tumbles down the rocky bed over a series of cataracts.

In 750m, you come to the picture-book hamlet of Smelthouses. Turn left and walk along the road, across the beck and then uphill for another 350m.

Just before a house, follow a bridleway to the left (SP Brimham). Walk up the concrete track past a small group of houses. At the far end, turn right off the track (SP Public Bridleway, Brimham). A green lane heads steadily uphill, and you can see the silhouette of Brimham Rocks on the skyline. In just over 1km, you come to a road. Turn left to reach the car park entrance after about 400m.

Yorke's Folly and Guisecliff Wood

Distance 8km **Time** 3 hours
Terrain wood and moorland paths; one
steep climb and care needed on cliff edge
Map OS Explorer 298 **Access** buses from
Harrogate to Pateley Bridge

A spectacular traverse of the edge of
Guise Cliff, with a visit to a 19th-century
folly perched on the edge of the moor.
The walk also explores the native
woodland of Guisecliff and saunters
alongside the Nidd for a pleasant return
to Pateley Bridge.

Leave Pateley Bridge by crossing the
bridge over the Nidd and passing the park.
Opposite the Royal Oak, bear left up the
side road towards Bewerley and walk
through the village. In just under 1km,
descend slightly to cross Turner Bridge
and come to a road junction. Turn right.
After about 300m, as the road begins to
rise, beyond the entrance to Skrikes Farm,

bear right to take a footpath and climb a
field (SP Nidderdale Way, Nought Moor).
At the top, go through a gate and keep
going up through Skrikes Wood. The path
meanders through some old quarries and
among oak trees, reaching a gate in the
wall at the top which gives access to the
open moor. Keep straight ahead on the
footpath beyond the gate and enjoy the
views back across Nidderdale and Pateley
Bridge. Keep rising, now through the
heather, for another 300m, to reach
another gate onto the road. Cross the road
and continue over the moor, aiming for
the two remaining ruined towers of
Yorke's Folly (SP Guise Cliff).

At the very least, Yorke's Folly is a grand
viewpoint. From here you can survey
most of Upper Nidderdale, looking down
on the wooded valley and far beyond. The
structure was built in the early 19th
century, an early job creation scheme for

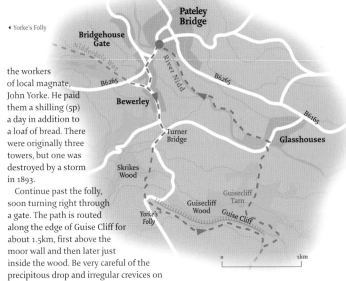

◄ Yorke's Folly

the workers of local magnate, John Yorke. He paid them a shilling (5p) a day in addition to a loaf of bread. There were originally three towers, but one was destroyed by a storm in 1893.

Continue past the folly, soon turning right through a gate. The path is routed along the edge of Guise Cliff for about 1.5km, first above the moor wall and then later just inside the wood. Be very careful of the precipitous drop and irregular crevices on the left, keeping to the narrow but distinct path. The views are excellent.

Pass to the right-hand side of a telecommunications mast, coming to a track. Turn left here and go through a gate just beyond the mast, leaving the Nidderdale Way which turns right on a track. The path goes steeply downhill, next to a wall on the right. After passing a stile in the wall, it curves round to the left, leaving the wall and dropping steadily down the hillside. Soon it levels out and passes through Guisecliff Wood, an area of shattered boulders, encrusted with moss and heather, at the base of the cliffs.

After a short rise, the path veers to the right and once again heads resolutely downhill, passing close to Guisecliff Tarn, which you may glimpse through the trees to your left. The path twists down through the woods and there are many side turnings. Ignore these and keep descending until you come to a gap in the wall at the bottom of the wood. Some steps lead onto a path, then a track. Pass the cottages and continue along the access track to a road. Turn left and then cross the Nidd. Immediately after the bridge, turn left along a track (SP Pateley Bridge). This makes for a nice unwinding saunter back to Pateley Bridge, passing a mill pond and fish farm on the way.

Industrial heritage of Greenhow

Distance 6km **Time** 2 hours
Terrain tracks and lanes, with short field
sections; the ford may be a challenge
after wet weather **Map** OS Explorer 298
Access Sunday DalesBus from York,
Ripon, Pateley Bridge and Grassington to
Greenhow (summer only)

Ancient and modern industry is visited
on this walk around Greenhow Hill and
Bewerley Moor, perched high on the
moors between the valleys of the Nidd
and the Wharfe. Like many areas in the
Dales, Greenhow was once a centre for
lead mining and the remains of the smelt
mills and mines haunt the upper reaches
of Brandstone Beck. Nearby is the
modern Coldstones Quarry and a
dramatic sculptured viewpoint.

   Start at the Toft Gate Lime Kiln car park,
1.5km east of Greenhow on the B6265

between Grassington and Pateley Bridge.
From the car park, cross a stile on
the opposite side of the main road
(SP Coldstones Fold). The public footpath
runs down several fields to reach a lane.
Turn right and continue downhill on the
tarmac towards the valley of Brandstone
Beck ahead. When the tarmac ends at
Coldstones Fold Farm, keep ahead on a
broad grass path, still descending. This
soon joins a farm access road which
continues all the way to a track junction
at the bottom of the valley.

   Turn sharp left, joining the Nidderdale
Way (SP Ashfold Side and Cockhill). On
approaching the house at Low Hole
Bottom, the Way turns sharp right,
crossing a ravine and beck and climbing
round the opposite bank through trees.

   For the next 700m the route lies
through level fields near the valley
bottom before coming alongside some
pretty waterfalls at Brandstone Dub. Cross
the stone bridge and slant up the far

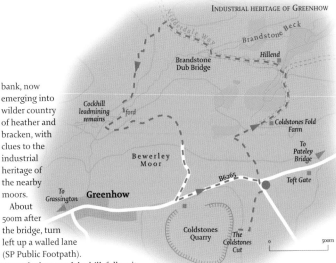

Map labels: Nidderdale Way, Brandstone Beck, Brandstone Dub Bridge, Hillend, Cockhill leadmining remains, ford, Coldstones Fold Farm, To Pateley Bridge, Bewerley Moor, B6265, Toft Gate, To Grassington, **Greenhow**, Coldstones Quarry, The Coldstones Cut, 0 — 500m

bank, now emerging into wilder country of heather and bracken, with clues to the industrial heritage of the nearby moors.

About 500m after the bridge, turn left up a walled lane (SP Public Footpath). Towards the top of the hill, follow it left and then right to climb over the brow through rough pasture land, before turning to the left. Down in the valley ahead lies the haunting detritus of historic lead mining. The smelt mill, spoil heaps and mining ruins of Cockhill crowd around the Brandstone Beck. The track ambles down to the beck, this time with no bridge to aid the crossing. A concrete ford is the alternative; after wet weather this may be quite deep. A little way beyond, in the heart of the remains, pass close to a modern stone building to the right.

From near here, follow a track turning sharp left and climbing up the valley side. It roams up the hillside, leaving the lead mining relics on the valley floor. Later, it becomes a tarmac lane and rises up to meet the main road close to the entrance to the modern quarry. Cross over the road and go through a gate into a bridleway running left, parallel to the main road (SP Permissive Bridleway, Peat Lane). Enjoy the views from this high vantage point across Nidderdale and arrive at the Toft Gate car park in less than 1km.

The impressive remains of the Toft Gate Lime Kiln are close by. It is also worth walking up the path to Coldstones Cut, about 500m from the car park. This feature comprises a maze of spiral walled paths twisting up to a viewpoint perched more than 400m above the vast hollow of the Coldstones Quarry. As a vantage point it offers panoramic views across the Dales to the west and the rolling countryside around Harrogate to the east. The 'golf balls' of Menwith Hill Early Warning Station may also glint in the distance.

◀ Cockhill

Ladies' Riggs and Ashfold Side

Distance 10km **Time** 3 hours
Terrain mostly good tracks and lanes,
some field paths **Map** OS Explorer 298
Access regular buses from Harrogate to
Pateley Bridge

**An interesting and varied circuit of two
subsidiary valleys of Nidderdale:
Brandstone Beck and Ashfold Side Beck.
Good tracks offer wide views across the
upper dale, but also provide glimpses
into the industrial history of lead mining
in the remotest parts of the moor.**

Leave Pateley Bridge by crossing the
bridge over the Nidd and passing the park.
Just beyond the petrol station and its
supermarket, turn right to follow a public
footpath. After 100m, turn right along a
road and very shortly turn left along a
track (SP Public footpath,
Ladies' Riggs). Head uphill,
with widening views over the
dale and Pateley Bridge.

Soon the track finishes at a house, but
keep straight ahead on a footpath,
climbing up the side of the hill on the
edge of fields. In about 1km reach a lane
and bear right to follow it. This is the
course of the Nidderdale Way, which
climbs along the crest of the ridge, Ladies'
Riggs. A while later, it drops through a
secluded valley, dotted with small
farmsteads and relics of historic lead
mining. Bend sharp right at Low Hole
Bottom to cross the beck as it scurries
through a deep ravine. Continue on the
track through trees and then along a level
section amidst fields. Pass the
picturesque waterfall at Brandstone Dub
and cross the beck. Slant up the far
bank, now moving into wilder
country. Remains of the
extensive lead mining
industry, which once
dominated this part of
the Dales, become

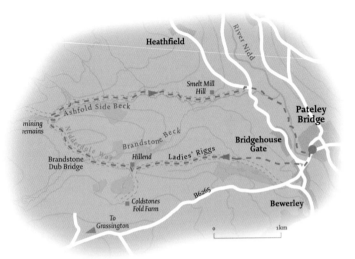

more evident. Keep on the track, over the crest of the hill but, as you descend towards the valley of Ashfold Side Beck, watch out for a public footpath sign turning left off the track. Follow this, dropping quite steeply through lead spoil heaps to reach a footbridge ensconced deep in the valley. This is the site of Providence Lead Mine, worked between 1781 and 1889. Today the lively beck tumbles down through the haunting remains of abandoned lead mines, cloaked with oakwoods.

On the far side of the footbridge, go through a gate and turn right, following a footpath slanting up the far side of the beck. Soon the path joins a track; follow this down to the right. It leads on along the slope of Ashfold Side Beck, heading towards Nidderdale. Further on it becomes a tarmac road, passing through a series of caravan sites, but still a very pleasant stroll along the waterside. Eventually, reach the road at a junction. Cross over, going through a gate on the opposite side and follow the footpath (SP Pateley Bridge). The path runs alongside the beck before crossing it on a footbridge. Walk across a field to join the raised banks next to the River Nidd. In about 400m, cross the river on a footbridge. Turn right on the far bank to walk along the riverside path into Pateley Bridge.

The Head of Nidderdale

Distance 15km **Time** 4 hours 30
Terrain mostly along tracks with some
steep climbs **Map** OS Explorer 298
Access no regular bus service to the start

Explore the wild uplands of the Head of
Nidderdale on this circuit to Scar House
Reservoir. The outward route contours
the hillside, encountering woods, fields
and moorland. Cross the dramatic dam
wall at Scar House before returning
across the moor on an old track. On the
way, How Stean Gorge gives an intriguing
insight into the geology and natural
history of the upper reaches of the dale.

Start at the small car park next to the
memorial hall in Lofthouse, reached via
the valley road from Pateley Bridge. Turn
right out of the car park and walk up the
road out of the village. Where the road
bends to the right, keep straight ahead
along a public bridleway (SP Scar House

Reservoir). The path traverses a series of
fields along the side of the valley, just
above the River Nidd. At first the route is
through woodland, but this soon opens
out. In 1.5km, pass through the buildings
of Thrope Farm. About 400m beyond
these, cross the riverbed, usually dry.
Climb along the base of a small gorge,
and then walk through the yard at Limley
Farm. Re-cross the dry bed of the river and
take the footpath on the other side as it
zigzags steeply up the bank. The path now
extends along the top of the bank, around
the grounds of Thwaite House, with a
wide panorama of Upper Nidderdale. Look
out for the line of the railway, built to
carry materials for the construction of
Scar House Reservoir and, in particular,
the tunnel portal that carried the route
through a spur on the corner of the valley.

An excellent track now contours around
the wide sweep of the dale as it curves

westwards into the high moors of the watershed. It passes the scattered houses and farms it serves and you get a first glimpse of the mighty Scar House Dam towards the head of the dale, backed by the whaleback of Great Whernside.

The access road ends at New Houses Edge Farm, but keep straight ahead onto the cart track, through a gate, still the Nidderdale Way. The path now crosses some fields and then veers right climbing up onto the hillside towards a shooting hut. A little way before the hut, turn left along the track, now level. This curves around the head of Twizling Gill, crossing the beck on a footbridge, and then around Woo Gill, this time fording the water.

The track continues for another 1.5km, before descending to Scar House Dam. Cross the dam and turn right on the far side. After about 300m, turn sharp left to stay on the Nidderdale Way, here known as In Moor Lane. There is a steep climb away from the reservoir now, affording great views across the head of the dale. Once the brow is reached, you can see ahead to Middlesmoor and the excellent track continues all the way to the village, about 3km distant.

Wind down through the houses of the village. At the bottom end, as you go round a sharp left-hand bend, take the footpath on the right, the Nidderdale Way. Follow this down a sequence of fields and a flight of steps to cross a wooden bridge over How Stean Gorge. This dramatic ravine has been gouged out of limestone by water and stretches for 1km at a depth of up to 20m. Climb up the other side and turn left along the lane, following this parallel to the gorge below. In about 500m, reach the entrance. There is a shop and café here and the chance to explore the gorge and its attractions (charge). The walk stays on the lane past Studfold campsite and activity centre, before reaching Lofthouse in another 1km.

◄ Scar House Reservoir

The Ribble rises in a remote area of upland
moor in the heart of the Yorkshire Dales.
Its source, near Ribblehead, lies close to
old routes into Wensleydale, Lunesdale
and Dentdale. The upper reaches of the
Ribble pass through exquisite limestone
country, with wide skies and the profile of
sculptured rocky peaks. The famous Settle-
Carlisle Railway Line accompanies the river
to find a high pass through to the Eden
Valley and on towards Scotland. Twenty
five arches carry the tracks over the moss at
Ribblehead.

The Three Peaks of Yorkshire preside over
the expanse of Upper Ribblesdale.
Ingleborough, Whernside and Pen-y-ghent
each have unique features to savour and
explore. Surrounding the Three Peaks is
country of great beauty and awesome
natural features such as Gaping Gill, Hull
Pot and the waterfalls of Ingleton.

Winskill ▶

Ribblesdale and the Three Peaks

Victoria Cave and Attermire Scar

Distance 6km **Time** 2 hours
Terrain hillside and stony paths
Map OS Explorer OL2 **Access** trains from
Leeds and Carlisle and buses from Skipton
and Kirkby Lonsdale to Settle

An extensive limestone plateau extends
eastwards from Settle towards Malham.
It is buttressed by steep crags rising
directly from the houses of the busy and
thriving town. The area richly rewards
exploration and this walk probes the
nature reserve of Attermire and
Langcliffe. The ceaseless action of water
has eroded the porous rock to mould
caves and fissures in the cliffs. One of the
most notable, Victoria Cave, is passed
along the way.

From the northern end of Settle Market
Place, go uphill past the Co-op and
continue ascending a narrow road (SP
Pennine Bridleway). Veer left on

Constitution Hill, soon leaving the town.
Further on, bear right, leaving the road to
continue on the Pennine Bridleway
(SP Langcliffe). A good walled track climbs
steeply uphill, with great views back over
Settle and across the Ribble floodplain.
Level out to follow a course just above the
enclosed land and on the edge of the open
moor, with limestone scars and rocks
puncturing the grass hillside.

Just before passing above the village of
Langcliffe, go through a gate and bear
right, leaving the village down below. It's
uphill again, rising diagonally across the
hillside and passing just below a small
wood. The sheer limestone cliff of Winskill
rears up ahead, with the Ribble's
meandering waters in the valley below.
The horizon features the flat top of
Ingleborough and, to the right, the great
dome of Pen-y-ghent. Pass through a gate

to reach a road, but don't follow it. Instead turn right (SP Pennine Bridleway, Settle Loop). A good track weaves gently up onto the limestone fell. In about 1km it bends to the left and you pass through a gate.

Immediately after the gate, turn sharp right, passing through a kissing gate into Langcliffe and Attermire Local Nature Reserve. The path follows the foot of the scar, just above a wall. A series of caves have been scoured out of the limestone. To reach Victoria Cave, leave the path about 300m after the gate and take a narrower trod bearing left up the hill. The cave is a great chasm into the face of the cliff and has apparently enjoyed a varied history. There are signs of animal habitation from around 12,000 years ago and evidence of its use as a shrine or workshop during the

Iron Age. Its name is hardly a cryptic clue to its rediscovery in the 19th century.

Returning to the main path, drop down between the buttress of Attermire Scar and the limestone hillocks of Warrendale Knotts to the right. Come to an expansive marshy hollow surrounded by hills.

At the bottom of the hill, at the path junction, turn right through a gap in the wall and cross a grassy hollow. Continue over a stile to head along the right-hand side of the wall, with the rocky hiatus of Warrendale Knotts towering to the right. The path passes through the gap in the hills and reaches a brow, with a panorama of Settle, the Ribble Valley and beyond opening out ahead. Descend steepening slopes to join the outward route. Turn left to return to Settle.

◀ Warrendale Knotts

Byways around Settle

Distance 6km **Time** 2 hours **Terrain** climb along a lane, then follow woodland tracks and riverside path **Map** OS Explorer OL2 **Access** trains from Leeds and Carlisle and buses from Skipton and Kirkby Lonsdale to Settle

Settle is undoubtedly a gateway to the Dales. Most walkers will head straight for the magnificent limestone uplands that beckon from the eastern fringe of the town. The southern environs of Settle are less well frequented, except by locals. Ancient woodland and quiet pastures offer a sense of remoteness and solitude, just a short distance from the bustling market town. A short walk explores this hinterland, climbing to a tranquil vantage point above the valley before returning alongside the river.

Settle repays exploration in its own right. The attractive market town sits between the Craven Faults, with craggy limestone hills

rising abruptly from the valley of the Ribble. The old road between West Yorkshire and the Lake District passes through the busy Market Place, a focus for visitors.

From the back of the Market Place, head to the right along High Street, passing the Talbot Arms, then continue on Victoria Street with the unusual and capacious Folly on the left. This 17th-century lawyer's *pied à terre* is now home to the Museum of North Craven Life. The road towards Airton and Kirkby Malham steers through the cottages of Upper Settle and then bears left to climb Albert Hill. Nearing the top of the town, bear right at a fork (SP The Pinfold). The lane is also the Pennine Bridleway and rises steadily for 1km. Pause to enjoy the views back over Settle, with the distant backdrop of Ingleborough.

When the road ends there is a fork. Bear right, staying with the Pennine Bridleway. The track follows the edge of a plantation for about 200m and comes to another

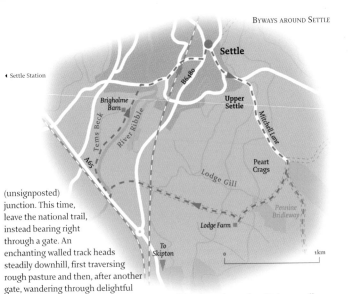

◄ Settle Station

(unsignposted) junction. This time, leave the national trail, instead bearing right through a gate. An enchanting walled track heads steadily downhill, first traversing rough pasture and then, after another gate, wandering through delightful woodland with graceful silver birch trees. Towards the bottom, the path crosses a gully. Immediately after this, turn right at a junction and go through a gate to pass the buildings at Lodge Farm. On the other side, a lane leads downhill with red campion, scabious and Herb-Robert decorating the summer hedgerows.

The track levels out as it passes Hoyman Laithe, but keeps straight ahead, ignoring the shortcut to Settle indicated by a fingerpost. There are wide views across the Ribble Valley until you cross the railway and arrive at the main road.

Take care crossing the busy road as the visibility to the left is limited. On the opposite side follow the small road signposted to Runley Mill. Continue past the mill towards the river. To cross the Ribble, leave the track and take a small footpath to the left, immediately before the bridge carrying the Settle bypass. On reaching the road, cross the river on the pavement and, on the far bank, take another footpath, to the right, leading back to the river bank. At the water's edge, turn left and follow the riverside path, now the Ribble Way. It may be a little overgrown at first, but this is short-lived and the path moves away from the main road. Head towards Settle, alongside the Ribble, a favourite spot for local ducks.

Continue along the riverside, through a number of fields and past a dairy. On reaching a road, turn right to return to the town, crossing Penny Bridge and passing the railway station, the start of the 116km-long scenic journey to Carlisle.

Smearsett Scar and Feizor

Distance 9km **Time** 2 hours 30
Terrain grass paths and tracks with some
lane walking **Map** OS Explorer OL2
Access bus from Settle to Stainforth

Just west of Stainforth, a fine ridge of
serrated limestone forms the distinctive
rocky outcrop of Smearsett Scar. This
landmark is the focus of a circuit that
uses two different routes connecting the
Ribblesdale village of Stainforth with the
charming hamlet of Feizor. On the way,
cross an ancient packhorse bridge and
savour wide views towards the west
coast. Return through ancient woodland
and pastures.

There is a pay and display car park just
off the main road in Stainforth. Follow the
path from the corner of the car park
(SP Pennine Bridleway) through an
underpass beneath the main road. On the
other side pass a small picnic area and

come to a gate. Follow the track to cross
the Settle-Carlisle Line and then continue
alongside the railway to meet a lane. Turn
left and follow the (very) minor road
(SP Little Stainforth) down to the river.
Cross the Ribble on the 17th-century
Stainforth Bridge.

On the far side, the lane passes a
caravan site and arrives at a crossroads
next to Knight Stainforth Hall. Keep
straight across here (SP Feizor). After a
short section of walled track, go through a
gate onto the open pastures.

The track bears right and then veers
left to climb the hill. There is no obvious
path for a while, but just maintain this
direction up the short-cropped pasture to
find a stile with a fingerpost next to a
gate. Once you reach the brow of the
hill, the distinctive rocky outcrop
of Smearsett Scar appears ahead, and on
the horizon the characteristic flat top
of Ingleborough.

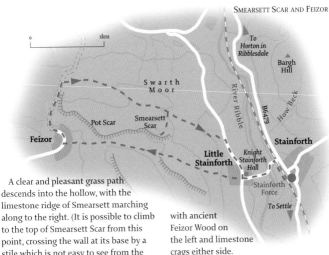

A clear and pleasant grass path descends into the hollow, with the limestone ridge of Smearsett marching along to the right. (It is possible to climb to the top of Smearsett Scar from this point, crossing the wall at its base by a stile which is not easy to see from the main path. Alternatively you can climb it on the return leg of the walk.) Rough pasture mingles with broken walls and limestone scree, with occasional hardy trees clinging to the edge. The views lie towards Lunesdale whose waters drain to the Irish Sea, for, although in Yorkshire, this is only a short way from the west coast and Morecambe Bay. The view also takes in the Forest of Bowland, not a forest but an area of remote upland that was once a royal hunting ground. A steeper descent down a grassy gully leads into the delightful hamlet of Feizor. Pass through a farmyard to reach a junction with a lane.

A welcome teashop lies opposite. Turn right here and walk along the lane through the village, curving left and winding up out of the settlement. It soon bends right again into a charming valley with ancient Feizor Wood on the left and limestone crags either side.

In about 1km, cross the brow of the hill and come to a wall and a gate with the dome of Pen-y-ghent and the lunar limestone of Moughton lying ahead. Just before the gate, turn right to take a footpath (SP Hargreave's Barn). It gradually ascends rough pasture towards the shoulder of Smearsett Scar. In 1.5km, just after the summit of the path, you can turn up to the right to climb to the top of Smearsett Scar. This avoids any walls and is a straightforward though quite steep route to the top. Returning to this point, continue across the stile and descend through enclosed fields, aiming for Hargreave's Barn, the ruined building next to a couple of large trees. At the road, turn right and follow it to the crossroads by Knight Stainforth Hall. Turn left, following the lane and your original route back to Stainforth.

◀ Smearsett Scar

45

A Ribbleside ramble

Distance 11km **Time** 3 hours
Terrain riverside paths and good tracks;
numerous stiles on riverside section
Map OS Explorer OL2 **Access** trains from
Leeds and Carlisle and buses from Skipton
and Kirkby Lonsdale to Settle

The landscape of the Dales is shaped by its
unique geology and in Upper Ribblesdale
it is the gritstone sentinels of Pen-y-ghent
and Ingleborough that preside over
everything. Between these iconic peaks
the Ribble weaves a course through
limestone meadows which are alive with
wildflowers in spring. This is a great
introduction to Ribblesdale, combining
riverside walking with a high-level
return across the meadows with their
panoramic views.

From the Market Place in Settle, follow
the main street north to cross the River
Ribble. Immediately after crossing the

bridge, turn right on the footpath – this is
the Ribble Way, signposted for Stackhouse.
Follow the path alongside and then above
the river until it reaches a lane, where you
turn right to follow the lane into the
hamlet of Stackhouse.

Immediately after the white house, turn
right (SP Ribble Way, Stainforth) to follow
a walled path back to the riverbank. Then,
with the weir ahead, turn left. For the next
2.5km, walk close to the water through
meadows and along higher wooded banks,
with a number of stiles. The path goes
between the campsite and the river,
passing the picturesque but treacherous
Stainforth Force, where the Ribble tumbles
down the North Craven Fault in a
spectacular series of rapids. Just after the
waterfall, you emerge onto a narrow lane
and turn right across Stainforth Bridge.
The narrow packhorse crossing was built
in 1675. Follow the lane uphill.

Stainforth

Stainforth
Force

Little
Stainforth

Catrigg
Force

◄ Stainforth Bridge

Stainforth
Scar

B6479

To
Malham

0   1km

Stackhouse

Ribble Way

Giggleswick
Scar

River Ribble

B6480

Langcliffe

Settle

When you reach the railway bridge, don't cross but turn right just before it to follow the Pennine Bridleway. Soon you go over the railway and under the main road to reach Stainforth village (toilets, pub, car park).

From the car park, follow the road into the village, turning right to cross Stainforth Beck, then immediately left, opposite the Craven Heifer pub (SP Pennine Bridleway). At a T-junction after 50m, turn left again, passing to the right of the village green. Then turn right once more, climbing steeply uphill on the Pennine Bridleway which soon becomes a walled track. As you climb, savour views left to Pen-y-ghent and Fountains Fell and behind to Ingleborough. At the top of the track, reach a gate. Before going through this, divert left down the steep footpath to

see the impressive spout of Catrigg Force before returning to the track. Go through the gate and continue up the track for this last bit of ascent before reaching another gate. Just through this, leave the track to bear right at the Pennine Bridleway sign to Winskill. The route is indistinct at first, but you soon pick up another track. At Upper Winskill, turn left, following the tarmac farm road across limestone meadow. There are now views right across Ribblesdale and Settle. At the T-junction, turn right to follow the road downhill for about 1km until it turns sharply to the right. At this point continue straight ahead through a gate, following the path back towards Settle. It's about 2km back to the town and the path gently descends across the hillside, skirting a wood and offering a relaxing vista of the dale and hills beyond.

Limestone country of Ribblesdale

Distance 13km **Time** 4 hours
Terrain tracks, lanes and limestone
pasture **Map** OS Explorer OL2
Access trains from Leeds, Settle and
Carlisle and bus from Settle to Horton

Horton is the most popular starting point
for the 40km Three Peaks challenge walk.
It sits astride the Ribble at the foot of two
of these peaks, Pen-y-ghent and
Ingleborough. This walk explores the
limestone country on the lower slopes of
both fells, including a wander through the
National Nature Reserve at Sulber.

Although there is a National Park car
park in the village, Horton is also the first
station on the Midland Railway's scenic
Settle-Carlisle Line, so there is a good
alternative to driving.

At the side of the Crown Inn, near the car
park, take the restricted byway signposted
for Birkwith. This is one of the ancient
tracks that cross the hillsides around

Horton, some of them old monastic
routes. The views are soon wide and
spectacular as the walled byway rises
directly from the village. All of the Three
Peaks can be viewed, with the profile of
Pen-y-ghent dominating the near horizon
to the east and the sprawling ridges of
Ingleborough rising to the west. In the
distance, to the north, the great wedge of
Whernside extends across the head of the
dale, its summit shared between Yorkshire
and Cumbria.

In about 2km, the track curves across the
bed of Sell Gill Beck, where any water
present disappears into deep sinkholes.
Pass through a gate and almost
immediately leave the main track, bearing
left to follow the Ribble Way, signposted
for Birkwith. Continue along a shelf above
the valley and just below a series of small
limestone scars. There are few waymarks,
but the route is clear enough. In a while,
join a track coming down from the right

and continue to a junction. Turn left on a broad track which winds down to High Birkwith.

Follow the signpost for Selside, passing Low Birkwith Farm (and ignoring a footbridge on the right) to continue through valley meadows alongside Coppy Gill. As you carry on, cross the infant River Ribble and on the far side curve round the left-hand side of the field to find a gate into a lane. This leads to Selside, a small railway and roadside hamlet; go under the railway to reach the main road.

Turn right and follow this for about 300m and, just after Top Farm, turn left up the wide walled track, which leads into an area of limestone pavement. This extensive rare karst terrain almost encircles Ingleborough with a series of scars, protected by an extensive nature reserve.

After 400m, there is a toll footpath straight ahead to Alum Pot, a large open shaft accessible only to experienced cavers and potholers. Keep with the main track, however, as it turns left here and stay on this until it ends at a gate. The bridleway continues, but is not obvious on the ground. To stay on it, keep walking in the same direction over well-drained turf across the next three enclosures. Towards the end of the third field, a grass track crosses the bridleway. Turn right along this and, after a few metres, go through a gate into the National Nature Reserve.

Just over 1km after entering the reserve, you come to a junction next to a fingerpost. Turn left here and follow this path, the main route between Horton and Ingleborough summit. It traces a route along Sulber Nick, a small notch in the limestone scars but also the line of a significant geological fault. It's a pleasant 3km walk back to Horton through limestone pavement and small crags. On the approach to the village take care when crossing the railway line.

Pen-y-ghent

Distance 10km Time 3 hours
Terrain exposed mountain route, rocky
climb to summit Map OS Explorer OL2
Access trains from Leeds, Settle and
Carlisle and bus from Settle to Horton

The outline of Pen-y-ghent dominates the
view from the Settle-Carlisle Railway as it
begins to climb north up the 'long drag'.
The mountain is one of the Yorkshire
Three Peaks and this route follows the
initial section of the 40km challenge walk.
The summit ridge is crowned by steep
crags that give the peak a rugged
grandeur. Its name reflects the Celtic
roots of the North West and means either
'Hill of the Border' or 'Hill of the Wind'.

From the car park in the middle of
Horton (charge) turn right and follow the
main road south, soon passing the famous
Pen-y-ghent Café, the traditional starting
point for the Yorkshire Three Peaks walk.
Continue along the road until just before
the church and the Golden Lion Hotel.
Turn left, taking the tarmac footpath
running just in front of the
boundary of the churchyard.
At the end of a field, pass
through a gate, descend the
steps and meet a lane.

Turn left and walk alongside the beck for
about 100m before turning right to cross it
on a footbridge. On the opposite bank,
turn left up the lane, past the school. A
brief woodland stretch soon gives way to
the familiar Dales landscape of small fields
and drystone walls.

In about 500m, as you approach the
hamlet of Brackenbottom, leave the lane
and follow the signpost for the summit.
The path climbs quite steeply up the side
of several enclosed pastures and later
negotiates a series of (avoidable) rocky
scars. The terrain is generally well-drained
limestone turf, though there are one or
two muddy places. The path continues
resolutely towards the distinctive façade of
Pen-y-ghent, its profile
resembling an
upturned ship.

Further up, the route has been upgraded with gravel and steps. Pause to enjoy the spectacle of Ribblesdale behind, perhaps with skylarks hovering overhead, and the flat top of Ingleborough as the backdrop.

About 2km after leaving the lane, the path reaches a T-junction and joins the Pennine Way. Turn left to begin the conquest of the summit. The path is very clear but also steep, with rocky steps and the occasional need for hands as well as feet; however, there are no great difficulties in reasonable weather. The final section is along a paved path.

From the trig point, there is an extensive panorama of the western side of the National Park, including Ingleborough to the west, Whernside to the northwest and Fountains Fell to the southeast. In poor weather the summit is very exposed. A compass or GPS is essential in misty conditions. Cross the gate/stile and leave the company of the wall, taking a rough path in a northerly, then NNW direction. Follow this to the edge of the summit plateau where a rough stone path drops down more steeply. About 1km from the summit, the path turns sharply to the left at a signpost, still the route of the Pennine Way and the Yorkshire Three Peaks. A well-surfaced path leads steadily downhill towards distant Ingleborough, later weaving its way through rough grassland, before coming to Tarn Bar, a junction of paths at the bottom of a small valley.

At this point, you may like to make a short detour to see the impressive natural pothole of Hull Pot. To do so, turn right and follow the grass track of the Pennine Bridleway for about 300m, then return to this point.

Otherwise, turn left for Horton in Ribblesdale, staying with the Pennine Way. A walled stone track leads back to Horton with Pen-y-ghent on the eastern horizon and the scenery making the gradual shift from limestone upland to rough pasture and valley meadows; the track reaches Horton in just under 3km. Turn left for a pint of tea at the Pen-y-ghent Café!

◀ Below Pen-y-ghent summit

Exploring Ribblehead

Distance 7km Time 2 hours
**Terrain tracks and field paths, mostly
quite level Map OS Explorer OL2
Access Ribblehead Station is served by
most trains on the Settle-Carlisle Line;
Sunday DalesBus to Ribblehead**

This route explores the classic limestone
scenery around Ribblehead where
becks disappear and reappear in an
amphitheatre of the porous rock,
surrounded by the highest peaks in
Yorkshire. It also takes in one of the most
photogenic features in the north of
England, the Ribblehead Viaduct.

From the Station Inn take the broad
stony bridleway towards the viaduct,
signposted for Gunnerfleet Farm. As it
approaches the viaduct you will notice
grassy embankments and other
earthworks to the right. This is the site of
the Ribblehead Locomotive Depot and

Brickworks, used in the construction of
the viaduct from 1869. At a junction of
paths where the broad track curves left
under the viaduct, take the path leading
right for Whernside. This is Blea Moor
Common, site of a temporary village
which housed the navvies who built the
railway. The path continues below and
alongside the viaduct. All of the Three
Peaks are clear from here: Ingleborough is
framed by the arches of the viaduct;
Pen-y-ghent dominates the southern
horizon, while Whernside rears up ahead.

Climbing alongside the tracks, the path
soon comes to a junction next to a
semaphore signal on the railway. The path
ahead continues to Whernside and you
may like to follow it for a short way to
view the isolated Blea Moor signal box,
but to stay on the bridleway, turn left here
and dive under the railway. On the far side
of the bridge continue through a gate. The

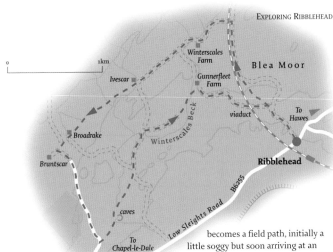

track meanders downwards, crossing Winterscales Beck and becoming a tarmac lane after the buildings at Winterscales. At a junction keep straight ahead to enjoy the lane which traverses a grassy terrace, just below a small limestone scar. Walk straight past the next farm buildings at Ivescar and pass just below the farm.

Keep straight ahead as the lane finishes, and continue on the bridleway. Cross a series of fields and pass the house and bunkbarn at Broadrake. Ignore the track to the left and in another 300m, you're joined by the Three Peaks path down from Whernside. Shortly afterwards turn left onto a lane, signposted for Hill Inn.

After 1km, the lane drops down to cross a beck but, immediately before the bridge, look out for a bridleway signpost to the left and follow a sunken footpath. This becomes a field path, initially a little soggy but soon arriving at an area of potholes, caves and limestone scars. The path makes its way across this area and crosses the beck, which is probably dry at this point. Climb the other side and continue along field paths until you meet a tarmac lane.

Bear left, now heading back towards the Ribblehead Viaduct. The farm road later crosses the Winterscales Beck, again likely to have been swallowed by porous limestone. After this bridge, it turns sharply right and soon forks. Go right, pass through a gate and head for the viaduct and Ribblehead. Approaching the collection of barns at Gunnerfleet, turn right to cross a bridge over Winterscales Beck, going past the barns and a house.

The track now winds under the viaduct to join the outward route. A few more steps returns you to the start and, if you like, the Station Inn, or possibly the regular tea van at the road junction.

Southerscales Nature Reserve

Distance 4km **Time** 1 hour 30
Terrain tracks and moorland paths, level
but squelchy in places **Map** OS Explorer OL2
Access Sunday DalesBus to Chapel-le-Dale

An extensive National Nature Reserve
almost encircles the northern and eastern
fringes of Ingleborough, the highest peak
wholly in Yorkshire. The reserve includes
limestone pasture and upland moors, but
it is the vast area of limestone pavement
that makes it particularly distinctive.
Within the reserve, at Southerscales, lies a
hidden limestone shelf located part of the
way up the slopes of Ingleborough yet
easily accessed from the road.

Worldwide this karst scenery is rare and
is formed by the weathering and erosion of
limestone to form clints (blocks) and
grikes (fissures) above a classic glaciated
valley. The porous rock also hides
immense underground watercourses and
caves, still not fully known.

Southerscales is located 7km northeast
of Ingleton, off the B6255. There is a small
roadside parking area about 300m

northeast (uphill) from the Hill Inn at
Chapel-le-Dale. From here, go through a
gate into the Ingleborough National
Nature Reserve (SP Ingleborough and
Great Douk). An information panel
outlines the important features of the
reserve. The track heads resolutely towards
the distinguished and shapely bulk of
Ingleborough. Pass an old lime kiln on the
left, giving an indication of the industrial
value of the lime here. A broad grassy path
leads along a level terrace on the hillside
with views down the wide valley of the
River Doe towards Ingleton and
Lancashire. In the distance, the hills of
Bowland brood over the horizon.

After 600m, come to a crossing of
paths. Keep straight ahead here,
enjoying the carpet of lovely
short turf. After the next
gate, you enter the
Southerscales Nature
Reserve. The path
begins to climb
into stony country
and you soon enter

another world, a wide expanse of bare rock pavement with stone slabs (clints) broken by deep crevasses (grikes). In this hidden upland shelf wildflowers grow in profusion, with scabious, harebells, tormentil and thyme growing near the path in season. In the grikes, thistles, hart's tongue fern, Herb-Robert, stunted thorn and ash trees colonise the scarce soil. As well as being a protected landscape, limestone pavement can be very dangerous, with leg-breaking fissures in the rock, especially risky in wet and slippery conditions. Towards the end of the pavement, on the left-hand side of the path is the deep abyss of Braithwaite Wife Hole. Soon after this, go through a gate to leave Southerscales.

Immediately afterwards, turn left (red waymark) and follow a narrow path next to the wall, leaving the main flagged path which continues as a very steep ascent to Ingleborough summit. You will notice the very marked change of terrain this side of the wall, having left the fertile, well-drained limestone grasslands for boggy, acidic peat that covers the harder sandstone and gritstone bedrock. Heather replaces rock-loving flowers. Cross a stile and then keep straight ahead at a wall corner, passing a small area of limestone pavement. Occasional semi-submerged flags ease the way across soggy sections,

but there is some unavoidable squelching.

The path gradually returns to drier limestone country, passing through a wall gap and then descending towards a patch of rough, undulating ground at the corner of a wall. Over the wall is the chasm of Great Douk Cave, the massive pothole enclosed by a wall and almost filled with trees. The sound of water echoes far below as the path curves left around the enclosure. At the bottom edge it widens and becomes clearer as it drops towards Chapel-le-Dale, reaching the crossing of paths on the outward route. Turn right to reach the start, or you can continue on the path ahead to drop steeply through fields to Chapel-le-Dale.

◀ Southerscales

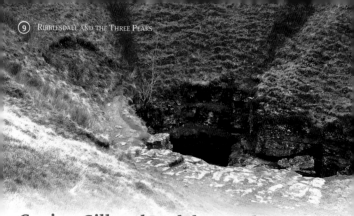

Gaping Gill and Ingleborough

Distance 14km **Time** 4 hours
Terrain stony tracks; beyond Gaping Gill,
exposed moorland and mountain
Map OS Explorer OL2 **Access** buses from
Settle and Kirkby Lonsdale to Clapham;
trains from Leeds and Morecambe to
Clapham Station, 2km from the start

An enthralling introduction to the
southern edge of the limestone country
of Craven, this walk follows a nature trail
through a woodland estate, visits the
beginning and end of one of the most
extensive cave systems in the North, and
climbs the best known peak in Yorkshire.
You can choose to turn back at Gaping
Gill to avoid the ascent of Ingleborough.

From the car park in Clapham, turn right
and walk up the lane, curving left to pass
the parish church. Cross the beck and turn
right to follow the lane to the edge of the
village. On the right is the entrance to the
Ingleborough Estate Nature Trail (modest
charge). Take this track as it zigzags up to

the lake and then follows an easily graded
route through the estate, suitable for all
abilities as far as the Ingleborough Cave.

The Nature Trail opened in 1970 to
celebrate the life of Reginald Farrer, who
collected plants from the Far East in the
early 20th century; the woodland is now
carefully managed. The ornamental lake
was originally used for a small electricity
generation system. Beyond the lake, the
path passes a nick in the rocks which
marks one of the geologically important
Craven Faults and the border of Dales
Limestone country.

In just under 2km, the track leaves the
wood, emerging into the upper valley of
Clapham Beck. Soon it passes the
entrance to Ingleborough Cave which
marks the end of a vast underground
system, carrying water from Gaping Gill,
2km to the north. The cave is open daily
from February to October and in winter by
appointment (charge).

Continue on the now rocky track. In

◀ Gaping Gill

500m, it turns sharp left as you approach the head of the dale where it enters the forbidding recess of Trow Gill, a deep cleft in the rocks between vertiginous walls. At the far end, a simple scramble brings the path out of the gill to follow a dry valley into the open moorland. In another 700m, it comes to a wall and ladder stile.

Cross the stile and continue on the path beyond, with Ingleborough presiding over the horizon ahead. A path to the right leads to Gaping Gill, one of the largest potholes in the UK. The waters of Fell Beck drop nearly 100m into the chasm and emerge at the entrance to Ingleborough Cave. The main path continues steadily up the southern slopes of Ingleborough.

A good path reaches the southern end of the plateau at Little Ingleborough, the upper section becoming rocky. Veer right across this subsidiary summit and head due north over the undulating plateau before a final climb to the top.

At 723m, it is the second highest peak in Yorkshire and a distinctive landmark for many miles. Remains of an Iron Age hillfort have been found here. The summit is a large flat area with the trig point towards the western edge. Care is needed with navigation and it is easy to choose the wrong route from the top. This walk returns by the outward route, so make a mental note of where it arrives on the plateau and use a compass if needed.

Return past Little Ingleborough and Gaping Gill to reach the ladder stile and the wall. Instead of returning along the valley follow the path ahead, bearing right across the moor. Soon this drops steeply into Clapham Bottoms, crossing the head of the dale and curving up the other side to the right to a gate. Here, you also join the bridleway from Ribblesdale to Clapham. Go through the gate and walk along the track, Long Lane, passing above Clapdale and the entrance to the cave. In 2.5km, at a T-junction, turn right. A walled lane drops back to Clapham, passing through a short tunnel on the way.

The secret valley of Kingsdale

Distance 10km Time 3 hours
Terrain tracks across limestone country,
with a few boggy sections
Map OS Explorer OL2 Access buses from
Settle, Kirkby Lonsdale and Lancaster to
Ingleton, 4km from the start

The valley of Kingsdale is a peaceful
sidetrack from the attractions of Ingleton
and the popular walks of the Three Peaks.
The valley has been carved by ice and is
now speckled with limestone scars and
boulders. This circuit of the dale offers a
high-level traverse along an old peat road
and an exploration of the valley itself.

To reach the start follow the road
towards Kingsdale and Dent from
Ingleton via Thornton in Lonsdale. Just
over the brow of a hill, watch for a
junction with a green lane on the right.
There are a few parking spaces here.

From the start, walk back uphill on the
road for about 300m. Turn right through a
gate onto a track, following it past a small
shed. The route winds on through rough
pasture, with limestone boulders and

scars peppering the hillside. After a fair
climb it levels out, squelching through a
short boggy section and then climbing
over the crest of the hill. As you gain the
brow the serrated profile of the Lake
District's highest peaks, including Scafell
Pike and the Coniston Fells, appear with
the intertidal sands of Morecambe Bay
completing the panorama.

About 1.5km after leaving the road, the
path comes to a track running parallel to a
wall. Turn right here to join the broad
track, known as the Turbary Road,
originally built to carry peat from the
slopes of Gragareth, higher up Kingsdale.

Enjoy this high-level traverse as you
head towards the massive wedge of
Whernside. There are extensive views
west to the Lakes and southeast as far as
Pendle Hill and the South Pennines. The
hill up to the left is Gragareth, crowned
with a series of cairns that could be
mistaken for human figures. The Turbary
Road runs along the boundary between
the porous limestone and the boggy peat
overlying sandstone and shale. This

◀ Rowten Pot

course reflects the original purpose of the peat road, but its line also means that it coincides with a sequence of potholes. The most notable is Rowten Pot, a collection of deep fissures created by a collapsed cave.

Carry on past Rowten Pot and go through two gates before the track parts company with the wall to take you across open moorland. Look out for a faint path, leaving the track and going downhill to the right, to the left of a small outcrop of rock. The way soon becomes clearer and descends a shallow reedy groove, passing through a gap in a stone scar and then aiming directly for a gate into the lane below. At the lane, turn left and follow the road for a short distance to visit Yordas Cave, a former Victorian show cave and the lair of Yordas, a child-devouring Norse giant.

Return to the road and, if you want a shortcut, keep going for 3km back to the starting point. Otherwise carry on to the signpost for Scar End and leave the lane for a tricky descent to Kingsdale Beck, which may well be dry. On the far side, cross the floodplain diagonally, aiming for a wood. When you get nearer, watch for a fingerpost in the wall and a stile just a little way short of an electricity pole. The path carries on towards the farmhouse driveway but just in front of it go through a gate, passing below the building.

Continue across the fields along the wall, then cross some squelchy country, with the limestone scars of Whernside's long south ridge above. Go over a stone stile in the corner of the enclosure and continue to another wooden stile to reach the end of the ridge known descriptively as Scar End. Relish the well-drained limestone turf and join a track coming down the ridge, which descends diagonally to join a green lane. Turn sharp right. This is the top section of Ingleton's popular Waterfalls Trail which leads back to the Kingsdale road and the start.

59

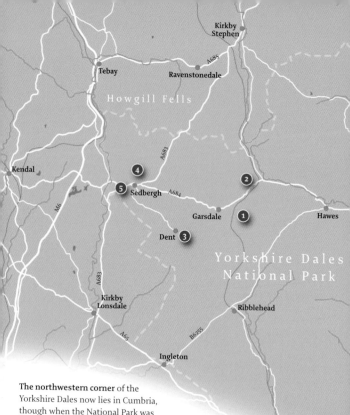

The **northwestern corner** of the
Yorkshire Dales now lies in Cumbria,
though when the National Park was
created this was part of the West Riding.
The expansion of the Yorkshire Dales
National Park brought in further areas
of Cumbria. These Western Dales are quite
different from their counterparts on the
eastern side of the watershed. The
Rawthey, Dee and Clough Rivers coalesce
near Sedbergh to feed the waters of the
Lune and the Irish Sea. Presiding over the

scene are the rolling hills of the Howgill
Fells, reminiscent more of the Southern
Uplands of Scotland than the Pennine
Dales. Sedbergh, the main settlement in
the area, lies at the foot of these appealing
hills. Dentdale is the most popular of
these valleys, with the unique and
intriguing village of Dent at its heart.

The Western Dales

Great Knoutberry and Arten Gill

Distance 10km **Time** 3 hours
Terrain lanes and tracks with some
moderate climbs **Map** OS Explorer OL2
Access trains on the Settle to Carlisle Line
to Dent

The Settle-Carlisle Line was the last
major railway line to be built in Britain
before the high-speed Channel Tunnel.
It was constructed by the Midland Railway
in the 1870s as an alternative to what are
now called the East and West Coast Main
Lines. The railway runs right up the spine
of northern England, passing through
some of the most grand and remote
landscapes in the country. One of its
notable features is the series of viaducts
built to cross some very challenging
terrain. This walk starts at the highest
station on the line (and indeed in the
whole of England) at Dent and passes
beneath one of the tallest viaducts.

Turn right out of the station approach
road and follow the lane, the 'Coal Road',
uphill. From the start there are glorious
views across Dentdale. After nearly 2km,
at a broad junction of tracks, turn right,
but first pause to admire the fantastic
panorama across the north of England.
To the west, the valleys of Dentdale and
Garsdale sweep down as they drain the
fells towards the River Lune. Beyond is
the serrated profile of the Lake District
fells. Northwards the broad and remote
heights of Swarth Fell and Wild Boar Fell
rise above Mallerstang and the
headwaters of the Eden.

Now the course of the Pennine
Bridleway, the track makes a wonderful
traverse around the flank of Great
Knoutberry, with views towards the flat
top of Ingleborough and the rising wedge
of Whernside. In 600m, turn left through a
gate to make the final ascent to the

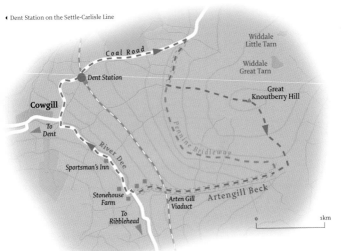

◀ Dent Station on the Settle-Carlisle Line

Coal Road

Widdale
Little Tarn

Widdale
Great Tarn

Dent Station

Great
Knoutberry Hill

Cowgill

To
Dent

Pennine Bridleway

River Dee

Sportsman's Inn

Stonehouse
Farm
To
Ribblehead

Arten Gill
Viaduct

Artengill Beck

0   1km

summit of Great Knoutberry, climbing the slope on a rough path by a fence. (If you prefer to omit the top of the hill you can just continue on the Pennine Bridleway, sweeping around its flank to join the Arten Gill Bridleway in just over 2km.)

Great Knoutberry's summit lies on the boundary between Cumbria and North Yorkshire and the main Pennine watershed. There were a number of small limestone quarries and associated kilns around the hillside, together with coal workings. Some remains are still evident. Pass the trig point and carry on alongside the boundary, soon veering right and descending the slope to join a track in just over 1km. This is the highest point on the pass between Widdale and Dentdale and the top of the Arten Gill Bridleway.

Turn right and head steadily downhill on the ancient walled bridleway, later passing under the massive arches of Arten Gill Railway Viaduct.

The track weaves through the small hamlet of Stonehouse, crosses the River Dee and reaches the valley road. During the 19th century, Stonehouse Marble Works was located here. In fact, it was not real marble, but a dark form of limestone that was prized for making fireplaces. Arten Gill Viaduct was also constructed from this local stone.

Turn right and follow this quiet lane, also the Dales Way, past the Sportsman's Inn at Cow Dub. In 2km, come to the hamlet of Cowgill and re-cross the River Dee. At the road junction turn right for Dent Station and Garsdale. The last 1km is a steep climb up the road to return to Dent Station.

Grisedale and Ure Force

Distance 8km Time 3 hours
Terrain moorland paths and tracks;
careful navigation required
Map OS Explorer OL19 Access trains
on the Settle to Carlisle Line to
Garsdale Station

This walk straddles the watershed
between Yorkshire and Cumbria on
the wild upland separating Garsdale
and Wensleydale. The tracks of the
Settle to Carlisle Railway thread across
the high moors, soon to begin the long
descent into the Eden Valley and
onwards to Carlisle.

Walk down the access road from the
station and cross the main A684 at the
junction. On the opposite side follow the
public footpath, signposted for Grisedale
and Flust. The path isn't very clear at first.
Avoid the temptation to follow a rough
track bearing right; instead walk up the
side of the rather soggy field on a faint
rising path, about 200m from the wall.
At the top of the enclosure, watch for a
fingerpost by a gap in the wall. Go

straight through, following the direction
of the signpost to climb the next field.
The path has now risen high above the
Grisedale Beck and there is a good view of
Clough Force waterfall below. Cross
another stile and keep straight on, now
aiming for the buildings at Blake Mire
ahead. Go to the right of the old
farmhouse and pass through a little gate.
Follow the fingerpost and some helpful
waymarker posts across the next boggy
fields. Walk just to the left of another old
barn and down to the ruins at Rowantree,
picking up a rough track and veering left
to reach the lane at Beck House.

Turn right along the lane, rising gently
through the remote and desolate country
of Grisedale, passing a small cluster of
houses and reaching the final dwelling,
East House, in just under 1km. A tarmac
track continues to climb steeply above the
house, soon bending sharply to the right.

Where the tarmac comes to an end, the
track bends back to the left at a rough
T-junction. Turn right at this point,
following the bridleway. The cart track

◀ Moorcock Inn, Garsdale

Map labels: Turner Hill, To Kirkby Stephen, Blades Farm, B6259, Ure Force, Moorcock Inn, To Hawes, Grisedale Beck, Clough Force, A684, Garsdale Head, Dandrymire Viaduct, To Sedbergh, Garsdale Station, 0 1km

soon disintegrates into a vague grassy path. Although a clear bridleway is marked on OS maps, it is not obvious on the ground and the next section requires care. You are aiming for a gate and stile; the grass path will take you too far to the right of this, so watch out for the stile on the horizon to your left, across some shake holes. Although the stile seems to crown an insignificant and squelchy rise, it marks the main east-west watershed of northern England. Behind lies Grisedale, feeding the Lune and the Irish Sea; ahead lie the headwaters of the Ure, running down Wensleydale and eventually flowing into the North Sea. Cross the stile and continue down rough pasture, reasonably close to a wall on your left, for about 700m. Aim for the bottom corner next to a house and then cross the railway by a footbridge. An access track then leads onto the road.

Cross the road and keep ahead on a good farm track towards Blades Farm, a change from the tufted moorland behind. In about 500m cross a bridge over the infant River Ure. Immediately afterwards, where the main track bends left to the farm, turn right along a rougher track.

Cross a beck and continue along the valley bottom for about 350m to meet the Pennine Bridleway. Bear right, soon passing the lovely waterfall at Ure Force. Shortly afterwards, turn right at a junction. Cross the River Ure and, about 100m further on, bear left off the main farm track. This is still the Pennine Bridleway, now on a grassy track, which leads to the Moorcock Inn.

Follow the Pennine Bridleway as it bypasses the road junction on a hardcore track, crossing first the B6259 from Kirkby Stephen and then the A684 towards Sedbergh. Once over both roads, continue on the track for Garsdale Station. It runs parallel to the railway and then dives beneath it, close to the impressive sweep of Dandrymire Viaduct. The bridleway meets the road just below the station.

Dentdale

Distance 7km **Time** 2 hours
Terrain riverside paths and lanes
Map OS Explorer OL2 **Access** Saturday bus
from Dent Station to Dent

**The River Dee stretches westwards
for nearly 16km from the heart of the
Yorkshire Dales to its confluence
with the Rawthey near Sedbergh.
Eventually its waters swell the River Lune
and in some ways Dentdale shares as
much in common with the Lake District
as the upland Yorkshire Dales. At the
heart of the dale is the lively and
picturesque village of Dent. This short
and mostly level walk offers a chance
to explore the village, the banks of the
River Dee and the pastoral surroundings
of Dentdale.**

The car park (charge) is opposite the
school at the western end of the village.

From here, turn left and walk along the
narrow, cobbled main street passing both
pubs, the Sun and the George & Dragon.
On the left there is a water fountain
commemorating Adam Sedgwick, one of
the pioneers of modern geology, who was
born in Dent in 1785. Keep on the road
towards Dent Station, passing around the
parish church of St Andrew and leaving
the village.

In another 300m come to Church Bridge
straddling the River Dee. The white painted
'WR' stone post is a reminder that
Dentdale, though now in Cumbria, was
part of the historic West Riding of
Yorkshire until 1974. Immediately before
the bridge, turn left through a stone stile
(SP Hippens), going down some steps and
following a pleasant riverside path. Dippers
flit across the river and chaffinches flutter
between the trees that colonise the bank.

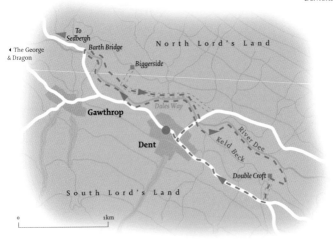

In 1km, rejoin the valley road and walk along this (right) for about 100m. Regain the path by bearing right through a kissing gate (SP Barth Bridge), again following the riverbank. The crags of Combe Scar loom above the valley to the left.

On reaching the bridge, turn right to cross the river and immediately afterwards turn right along a lane (SP Not suitable for HGVs and liable to flooding). This is a quiet hedged lane but, as the sign warns, it is vulnerable to overspill from the adjacent river in the form of large puddles or flooding. Primroses, violets and bluebells are among the wildflowers gracing the hedgerows in season. In about 1.5km, watch for a waymark in the wall to the right indicating a shortcut across the meadow to Church Bridge. If you miss this, you'll arrive at the bridge anyway in due course.

Cross the bridge, arriving at the point where the outward route left the road. Instead of returning directly to Dent, the walk can be extended by turning left after the bridge, now back on the south side of the River Dee. After about 200m, cross a concrete bridge over the Keld Beck and continue on the Dales Way, soon beside the River Dee once more. Keep to the riverbank for about 1km. Pass some stepping stones in the river, carrying on along the bankside footpath, which soon leaves the Dee to continue alongside Deepdale Beck. About 200m after the confluence of these two watercourses, leave the riverside path to turn right through a gate and walk through a field to the farmhouse at Double Croft. Turn left up the concrete track, which soon reaches a road. Turn right and follow the lane back to Dent.

The ascent of Winder

Distance 6km **Time** 2 hours 30
Terrain steep ascent and exposed high-
level walk on good paths, but a compass
is needed in mist **Map** OS Explorer OL19
Access bus from Kendal to Sedbergh;
summertime weekend bus from Dent
Station to Sedbergh

The town of Sedbergh dates from
Norman times and the remains of the
motte and bailey castle can be seen as a
mound just to the east. Sedbergh School
originated as a chantry school in 1525 and
its buildings spread across the south side
of the town. Today Sedbergh has a
reputation as a 'book town' with a
number of second-hand booksellers in
the area. It is a pleasant and interesting
centre, lying just above the Rawthey
Valley, at the foot of the rounded green
Howgill Fells. The first of these, Winder,
presides over the town and presents a
steep challenge.

From the car park at Joss Lane in
Sedbergh, turn right and walk along the
main street. Just after the Dalesman
Country Inn, turn right up Howgill Lane,
climbing out of the town and passing the
People's Hall, some splendid Victorian
villas and the community recreation
ground. As you leave the town, at the end
of a housing estate, watch out for a right
turn. Leave the road here, bearing right
along the farm access road (SP Permissive
path to the Fell). Walk up to the farm,
passing to the right of the buildings,
through some gates and then onto the
open fell.

Turn left and follow a broad track
diagonally up the hill next to the wall.
Maintain this direction when the wall
changes course. Continue for another
500m, until a broad grassy path swings
more directly up the slope. It rises steeply
to the brow and then veers right along the
ridge to arrive at the summit. A trig point

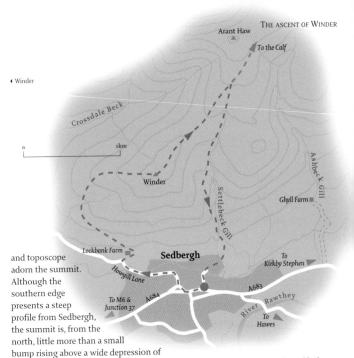

and toposcope adorn the summit. Although the southern edge presents a steep profile from Sedbergh, the summit is, from the north, little more than a small bump rising above a wide depression of exposed moorland. Beyond this the land rises more steadily to the highest peaks of the Howgills.

From the summit, keep straight ahead, the path gradually descending across the moor (soggy in places). In about 1km you reach the bottom of the moorland depression. Go on for another 150m, climbing gradually, and watch out for a path on the right. The junction is on a level section, just before a steeper ascent. If you want to climb all the way to the summit of the Howgills, keep on the path to skirt Arant Haw and then climb up to

Calders and eventually to The Calf. There is a good path for most of the way, but from Calders to The Calf the terrain, though easy, can be confusing.

Unless you want to extend your walk in this way, turn right at the junction and follow the path descending the flank of Winder, above the course of Settlebeck Gill. After 1.5km, go through a kissing gate and continue on the path, with the gill and gorge to your left. At the bottom go through another gate and emerge onto Joss Lane, bringing you back into Sedbergh.

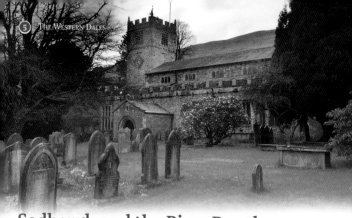

Sedbergh and the River Rawthey

Distance 10km **Time** 3 hours
Terrain green lanes, riverside and field
paths; two short sections of main road
Map OS Explorer OL19 **Access** bus from
Kendal to Sedbergh; summertime
weekend bus from Dent Station
to Sedbergh

The ancient parish of Sedbergh spread
for more than 50,000 acres along the
valleys of the Rawthey, Dee and Clough,
their waters eventually swelling the
Lune. This was both a centre for hand
knitting and the cradle of the Quaker
movement. George Fox preached in the
area and one of the oldest meeting
houses is in Brigflatts. This walk explores
Sedbergh's hinterland, following the
River Rawthey and the lower slopes of
the town's own hill, Winder.

From the car park at Joss Lane, turn left
to go along the main street for about
200m, then cross the A684. Walk along
Vicarage Lane (SP Millthrop and Settle

Beck), passing a small housing estate.
Where the lane turns left, keep straight
ahead through a kissing gate and follow
the path up the field, crossing another
drive. Just after a boarding house for
Sedbergh School, the path splits. Bear
right, go through a small gate and follow
the path as it curves right, descends a
bank and reaches the road.

Turn left and follow the road for about
300m. Just before it crosses the river, turn
right (SP Birks). The path continues near
the river for 1km, at first along a small
ridge just above the Rawthey, with views
across to Sedbergh and its school. Go
through a wood and then continue nearer
the river until you climb up to the left of
Birks House to meet a lane.

Again turn left and pass through the
hamlet of Birks, following the lane
downhill past a factory. Watch out for a
small riverside path (SP Dales Way). This
wanders along an elevated wooded
terrace, a little way above the swirling

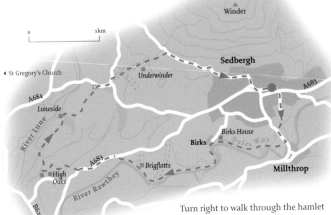

◄ St Gregory's Church

waters of the Rawthey. Continue alongside the river for nearly 2km, passing its confluence with the Dee, coming in from Dentdale. The path continues under the remains of an iron bridge that carried a railway over the river. This line left the Skipton-Lancaster route at Clapham and joined the West Coast Main Line in the Lune Gorge to the north. Later, pass the small settlement of Brigflatts, though there is no access from the footpath. To visit the historic Quaker Meeting House, you need to take the direct path from Birks.

Reach the A683 and turn left. A footpath leads alongside it for about 400m, but then there's no pavement so take care on this busy road. Watch for a footpath on the right, through a gate (SP High Oaks). This is still the Dales Way and crosses Haverah Beck at the end of the field. Bear left across the next field, then along a green lane to the houses at High Oaks.

Turn right to walk through the hamlet and then turn right again, staying with the Dales Way along a green lane (SP Killington Bridge, Lincoln's Inn Bridge). In 300m, as the green lane ends, bear right (SP Lincoln's Inn Bridge). When the path splits again, follow the sign for Luneside, soon taking another green lane. At Luneside, leave the Dales Way, and keep right to take the access track from the farm buildings. In 700m, come to the main road next to St Gregory's Church, no longer used for regular public worship.

Taking great care, turn right to follow the main road for about 200m. Go left up a minor road and, almost immediately, bear right across a cattle grid to take a farm access road towards Underwinder – against the splendid backdrop of the Howgill Fells. On the approach to Underwinder, bear right through a gate, following the footpath sign. Climb the next two fields to meet a lane. Turn right to return to Sedbergh.

Wensleydale is broader and more pastoral than most of the other valleys in the Yorkshire Dales. Its river, the Ure, rises near Garsdale Head on the border with Cumbria. The wide and relatively fertile floor of the dale has made it a centre for dairy farming and the famous cheese is made locally. Along the valley, a string of interesting and homely settlements provide great centres for exploration, from Hawes at the head of the dale to Leyburn and Middleham further down. The Ure cascades down a sequence of attractive waterfalls at Aysgarth, while the side valley of Raydale cocoons the tarn of Semer Water.

Swaledale is the most northerly of the major Yorkshire Dales. The river follows a deep and sinuous course from Keld to Richmond, with a variety of interesting side valleys such as Gunnerside Gill and Arkengarthdale. Lead mining has left its mark here, more than almost anywhere else in the Dales. The remains of this 19th-century mineral bonanza leave a fascinating trail of industrial archaeology in this remote and harsh upland country.

This terrain also offers fantastic walking country with long trackways stretching across the moors and between the dales. The upper reaches of Swaledale are the furthest areas of the National Park from major centres of population. Once you leave the most popular spots, you will probably only have sheep for company.

Towards Keld ▶

The Northern Dales

The highest fall in England

Distance 7km **Time** 2 hours 30
Terrain meadow paths **Map** OS Explorer
OL30 **Access** buses from Leyburn and
from Garsdale Station to Hawes

Hawes is an attractive market town set in
the wide pastures of upper Wensleydale.
There is no shortage of pubs, cafés and
shops. Small hamlets and settlements
are scattered across the glaciated scenery
and this walk uses meadow paths to visit
two of the most attractive, Sedbusk and
Hardraw. Along the way, it also explores
two contrasting ravines, carved out of the
bedrock by the force of Hardraw Beck: the
first, Shaw Gill Wood, is a hidden gem, off
the main tourist routes; the second is the
dramatic cascade at Hardraw Force.

The main car park in Hawes is the site of
the railway that ran the length of
Wensleydale, joining the Settle-Carlisle
Line at Garsdale. It is also home to a

National Park Centre and the Ropemaker
visitor attraction. From the car park, walk
through to the main road and then take
the side road north towards Hardraw – at
this point also the route of the Pennine
Way. Cross the old railway and, shortly
afterwards at a road junction, find a path
bearing left, remaining with the Pennine
Way. A paved way crosses the fields to
rejoin the road at the far side of a loop.
Continue along the road, crossing the Ure
by Haylands Bridge. In a further 250m,
leave the road to take a footpath to the
right (SP Sedbusk). Cross a ditch and
climb the next two fields to reach a road.

Cross over, climbing a stile on the
opposite side, and walk across the next
three fields, arriving at a lane. Turn right
and walk into the hamlet of Sedbusk. The
hamlet consists of an eclectic variety of
houses, mostly dating from the 18th
century. Its position, hidden away on a

◀ Hardraw Force

Shaw Gill Wood

Hardraw Force

Simonstone Hotel

Hardraw

Sedbusk

Hardraw Beck

Pennine Way

Floshes Hill

Shaw Gill Wood

River Ure

Hawes

To Aysgarth

A684

0   1km

narrow lane on the lower slopes of the valley, adds to its charm.

Turn left by Chapel Cottage and walk past the village green. Almost at the end of the green, turn left (SP Simonstone) to pass between the houses. The path crosses a sequence of small, walled enclosures just above the valley floor. Eventually it comes to a road. Turn right here, and walk along the road for about 350m, past Simonstone Hall. As it bends to the right before a couple of houses, turn left (SP Shaw Gill Wood). A cobbled lane drops down to reach the wooded valley floor, close to a footbridge. There are footpaths on both sides of the gill and a bridge at the far end, so you can make a circuit by going either way round – Hobson's choice! Either way, it is a charming wooded clough, well worth the exploration.

Return to the road and retrace your steps to Simonstone Hall. Turn right through the 'exit' of the car park and keep ahead on a footpath (SP Hardraw). A track leads to a house and the path then passes to the right of the building and steeply down towards Hardraw, arriving at the Green Dragon. There is a toll to visit the waterfall at Hardraw Force. To reach this, you pay at a machine or at the heritage centre behind the pub. The centre includes pictures and information about the area and also has a café. An attractive path leads from here into a hidden gorge curving round to a wall of rock. The water thunders over the cliff in a dramatic spout. At more than 30m in height this is the longest single drop in England.

Returning to the Green Dragon, take the footpath opposite, just in front of the bridge over the beck (SP Hawes). Once again on the Pennine Way, continue across the valley floor to meet the road after 1km. Return to Hawes by your outward route.

The mysterious charm of Semer Water

Distance 8km (shortcut 6km)
Time 4 hours (shortcut 3 hours)
Terrain lakeside paths, then steep ascent and exposed moorland **Map** OS Explorer OL30 **Access** no public transport to the start

This is a circuit of two distinct parts. The outward route lies along the water's edge and across the marshy fringe of the lake. The return climbs steep and exposed moorland with grandstand views, though you can avoid this by a more level shortcut along a quiet lane.

The origin of Semer Water is told by a legend which recounts how a homeless man was once refused hospitality by all but one household in the prosperous valley. Turning into an angel, the erstwhile beggar cursed the grudging community, saying 'Semerwater rise, and Semerwater sink, and swallow the town all save this house, where they gave me food and drink'. Thereupon, the community was flooded.

Less prosaically, Semer Water was formed by glacial action at the end of the last ice age. It is one of only two significant natural lakes in the Yorkshire Dales; the other is Malham Tarn. Much of the lake is shallow and there is an extensive curtilage of wetland, attracting waders and other birds. The southern end of the lake is protected as a nature reserve; willow, sedge and water lily thrive here.

Start at the crossroads in Countersett, 4km along a minor road running south of Bainbridge. There are a few parking spaces on the roadside nearby. Follow the road downhill towards the outflow of Semer Water (SP Stalling Busk). The bridge at the bottom marks the start of the River Bain's short journey to join the Ure at Bainbridge.

Pass a jetty, landing areas and the board which records where J M W Turner sketched for a painting in 1816. Soon afterwards, as the road begins to climb uphill, opposite farm buildings, turn right to cross a stile. Although initially boggy

◀ Ruined church by Semer Water

the path skirts the lakeside just above the water's edge and then leads to the former parish church of Stalling Busk, dating from the 18th century. The church was abandoned in 1909, but the building was restored at the end of the 20th century. Although disused as a place of worship, about 750 people are buried in the churchyard.

Just beyond the ruined church, the path divides. The left-hand fork goes to the village, but this walk bears right for Marsett. The distant view looks towards the head of the dale, with small enclosures, dotted with barns, rising to the open fellside above. Continue across the fields and stiles, ignoring any side options, until you meet a track. Turn right, cross the beck and follow the track beyond along the left-hand side of the water. When it becomes submerged in a long ford, pick a route along the left bank until it emerges on the far side.

A stony causeway makes for easier going across the marsh and a footbridge to the left avoids a second ford. This area is part of Semer Water Nature Reserve and the rocky track weaves alongside the Marsett Beck into the hamlet of Marsett, the highest settlement in the dale.

At the road, turn right, crossing Marsett Bridge, then soon leave the road for the track signed for Burtersett and Hawes. (For a shorter and direct return to Countersett, continue along the quiet lane, passing above Semer Water.) When the wire fence ends, take a footpath waymarked to the right, crossing a stile. It climbs steeply, initially by a wall. On reaching the crest of the ridge, you come to a bridleway, marked by a fingerpost.

To the left, from here, you should be able to see a broad stony track climbing a hill in the distance. This is known as Cam High Road, a Roman road crossing the watershed above Bainbridge on its way to Lancaster. Having looked, turn right along the ridge path. In about 1km, this bears right and descends to the road. Turn right to return to Countersett.

Askrigg and Mill Gill

Distance 5km **Time** 2 hours
Terrain narrow paths in gill, returning by track and field paths **Map** OS Explorer OL30
Access no public transport to the start

Stone cottages, shops and houses line Askrigg's long main street, sloping up from the 15th-century parish church of St Oswald. Once known for its clockmakers, it has more recently been the home of 'Skeldale House' for the TV series *All Creatures Great and Small*. A short way from Askrigg lies the secretive Mill Gill, a wooded ravine spawning two waterfalls. Named after the mill at its foot, Mill Gill Force drops 7m over a rocky parapet in the depths of the wood. Further up is the hidden Whitfield Gill Force. This walk explores the falls before returning along a high-level track and field paths.

To reach Askrigg, turn off the A684 at Bainbridge. There is parking available next to the church, with an honesty box for payment. Take the road on the upper side of the parish church (SP Mill Gill Force). Walk through to the end of the village and, opposite Flax Mill, watch for a footpath to the right. Go through a small gate to walk along a flagged footpath, crossing a field diagonally.

Continue past another old mill into the woods beyond and then follow the path alongside Mill Gill, which has carved a small gorge through the bedrock. Soon, cross a footbridge and walk through another small field. Return into the woods and climb steeply up above the beck, with a near vertical drop down to the water.

In about 500m, come to a fingerpost which indicates a short cul-de-sac path to

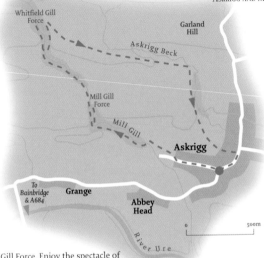

Whitfield Gill
Force

Garland
Hill

Askrigg Beck

◄ Mill Gill

Mill Gill
Force

Mill Gill

Askrigg

To
Bainbridge
& A684

Grange

**Abbey
Head**

River Ure

0   500m

view Mill Gill Force. Enjoy the spectacle of the sylvan cascade before returning to the junction, then continue up the main path (SP Whitfield Gill). Climb through the woods and skirt the fields, before returning to the trees with ash and silver birch clinging to the steep slope. Cross a bridleway in a clearing and continue ahead until you reach a fork.

To view Whitfield Gill only, take the left-hand option and walk on for about 350m, then return to the fork. To continue on the main circuit, follow the right-hand fork (SP Askrigg via Low Straights). The path descends, crossing a paved section and then a footbridge, where the beck tumbles through a deeply recessed wooded gorge.

Climb steeply up the far bank, with steps aiding the way. The path then heads through beechwoods, along the edge of the ravine, before arriving at a green sward with thoughtfully placed seats.

Go through the gates between the seats, on a path leading to Low Straights Lane. Turn right here and head downhill, an archetypal Dales walled lane with a panorama of Wensleydale at your feet. In about 1.5km, immediately before a forded footbridge over the Askrigg Beck, turn right to follow a footpath (SP Askrigg). This drops down through fields, initially keeping to the right-hand side high above Askrigg Beck. There are no further signs; just watch out for the stiles and gateways as a guide to the route. The right of way emerges near the top of the main street with a short walk back to the church and some cafés and pubs to tempt you to linger.

Aysgarth Falls and Bolton Castle

Distance 12km **Time** 4 hours 30
Terrain mostly field paths with no
serious climbing **Map** OS Explorer OL30
Access buses from Leyburn and Hawes
to Aysgarth

Might and force is the theme of this walk,
but in very different senses. At Aysgarth
the force of the River Ure is evident as it
cascades over a series of rock ledges to
create three separate waterfalls. A short
distance away, the towering ramparts of
Bolton Castle are a reminder of martial
power. The castle was built in the 14th
century and Mary Queen of Scots was
imprisoned here for six months in 1568.
The two locations are linked through a
network of field paths and tracks,
offering a great insight into the farming
landscape of Wensleydale.

Start from the National Park car park in
Aysgarth, where there is a café and toilets.
(To reach, it turn off the A684 at Aysgarth
and head towards Carperby.) Cross the
road and enter the nature reserve
opposite, taking the footpath. You can

view the Middle Force by going down
some steps to the observation platform.
The broad main path stays ahead through
Freeholders Wood. Be alert for a fork in
the path and bear left here (SP Castle
Bolton) to continue through Freeholders
Wood and Riddings Field, a local nature
reserve. Leaving the woodland, climb up
the meadows and pass the farm buildings
and Hollins House. Walk along the
driveway for a short way before taking a
footpath to the right across a field
(SP Castle Bolton). At a wall crossing, a
fingerpost gives you a choice of routes to
Castle Bolton.

Continue straight ahead here, towards
High Thoresby Farm, following the track
as it veers to the right in front of the farm
buildings and then passes a barn. After a
short walk along the farm approach drive,
bear right to leave it, and follow a
footpath diagonally through a
meadow. It crosses a small dell

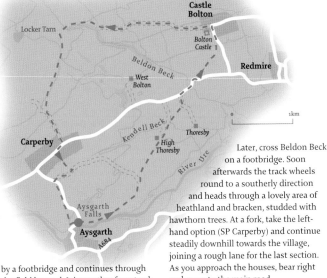

Later, cross Beldon Beck on a footbridge. Soon afterwards the track wheels round to a southerly direction and heads through a lovely area of heathland and bracken, studded with hawthorn trees. At a fork, take the left-hand option (SP Carperby) and continue steadily downhill towards the village, joining a rough lane for the last section. As you approach the houses, bear right and come to the main road.

Turn right and follow the road for about 200m before turning left onto a footpath opposite the Wheatsheaf pub (SP Low Lane). Continue across grass meadows for about 400m, ignoring side turnings until you come to a walled lane. Turn right to follow Low Lane until it reaches a road. Turn left, but in 50m go through a small gate on the right-hand side. This gives access to a public footpath, at first running next to the wall and later descending through parkland to cross the line of the old Wensleydale Railway. A flight of steps leads down to the National Park car park at Aysgarth and you will probably hear the waters of the Aysgarth Falls as you approach.

by a footbridge and continues through the field beyond. Join another farm track to reach the road. Turn right and walk along the road for 500m, taking care as it is quite busy and dangerous. Where it bends sharply to the right, take a footpath to the left, through meadows. Emerge at the top of a sunken lane. Turn left, past the houses and up their access drive. At the top, a road leads up to Castle Bolton.

At the castle, turn left, passing St Oswald's Church and the car park. From here take the farm track (SP Askrigg) as it runs westwards along the slopes of Wensleydale. Enjoy wide views across the dale. In 1.5km pass between farm buildings. Further along, weave through a small plantation and cross a little beck. This may need a jump if it's in spate.

Castles and Gallops of Middleham

Distance 4.5km **Time** 1 hour 30
Terrain fields and heathland
Map OS Explorer OL30 **Access** bus from
Leyburn and Richmond to Middleham

There are two castles in Middleham. The original fortification was a wooden motte and bailey affair, on a site now known as William's Hill. The present stone structure replaced it in the late 12th century and was, for a time, the home of Richard III. It dominates the town and surrounding landscape, crowning the low ridge between the Ure and Cover. Middleham is also known for its links with training racehorses and the walk passes the 'Gallops' on Middleham Low Moor. In between lie the tranquil wooded banks of the River Cover.

Middleham is an interesting historic town, with lots of character. There is plenty of parking around the town squares and it is replete with pubs and cafés. From the square, go a little way up the Coverham road and turn left at the snicket, to the right of the Castle Keep Tea Rooms. This leads directly through to the castle. Take the lane and along the left-hand side of the castle keep (SP Footpath), which leads to a gate at the edge of the town. If you have time, you could take the footpath bearing right to climb William's Hill, a motte and bailey fortification.

Otherwise, carry on straight ahead through the gate and along the edge of the field to climb over a low spur between Wensleydale and Coverdale. Look back for good views over Middleham Castle and across Wensleydale to the hilltop market town of Leyburn. At the end of the first field, go through a gap and then continue along the next enclosure, with the wall on

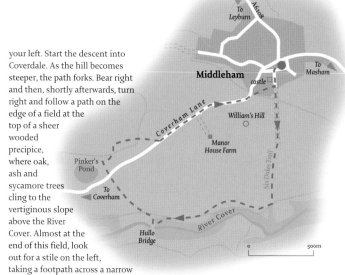

your left. Start the descent into Coverdale. As the hill becomes steeper, the path forks. Bear right and then, shortly afterwards, turn right and follow a path on the edge of a field at the top of a sheer wooded precipice, where oak, ash and sycamore trees cling to the vertiginous slope above the River Cover. Almost at the end of this field, look out for a stile on the left, taking a footpath across a narrow spike of woodland and over a couple of stiles. Continue gently downhill, crossing the pasture beyond, before descending steeply to meet the river close to Hullo Bridge.

The river has carved a shallow gorge through the bedrock and flows swiftly downstream towards its imminent confluence with the Ure. Green woodpeckers cackle through the trees and if you're lucky you may catch the fleeting turquoise sheen of a kingfisher. Linger on the bridge and enjoy the moment, but don't cross it. Instead, stay on the north bank, climbing a gently rising diagonal path among thistles and hawthorn trees.

On reaching a road, cross and continue on the other side, through the grassy area, also used as an informal car park. Follow a broad grassy track to the right of Pinker's Pond and on up the bank towards an old quarry. Turn right before the quarry and then bend left to meet a hardcore track. The broad expanse of Middleham Low Moor and the Gallops now lies ahead. Turn right to follow the track, called an equine walkway and used by horses. Cross the road again, turning left and walking along the wide verge. Where the verge stops, go through a gate on the right-hand side to follow a public footpath (SP Middleham). A sequence of fields brings you to the back of the castle. Turn left and follow the track back into town.

◄ Pinker's Pond

83

Marske and Telfit Bank

Distance 7km **Time** 2 hours
Terrain farm tracks and a quiet lane; one
significant climb **Map** OS Explorer OL30
Access no public transport to the start

Marske Beck is a tributary of the Swale,
draining a huge area of heather moor
extending to the watershed with the
Tees. Like many areas of Swaledale, the
moors have been exploited for lead and
other minerals, but today their main use
is for sheep, cattle, grouse and
pheasants. This walk explores the lower
valley of Marske Beck, with a tantalising
glimpse into the wild uplands between
Yorkshire and County Durham.

Marske lies 8km west of Richmond, just
north of the A6108. It has strong
connections with a 17th-century
Archbishop of York, Matthew Hutton,
who bought the estate in 1596. The
present hall, a Georgian building, lies a
short way from the start of the walk and

can be glimpsed through an ornamental
gateway. The beck passes through the
grounds which include ornamental
gardens, fishponds and woodland.

There are a few parking spaces by the
bridge at the bottom of the village. From
here, walk up the road into the village,
passing below the parish church. The
Norman church is dedicated to
St Edmund the Martyr and was restored
in 1683. Just beyond, at the road junction,
turn left, going past a postbox and
heading straight ahead to reach a broad
track and bridleway.

This leaves the village, contouring
across the bank, above the valley. Carry on
past the former chapel and houses at
Clints and enter the mixed forestry of
Clints Wood. Stay on the track, ignoring
side turnings. Later, where it splits,
continue straight ahead on the lower
branch, soon arriving at a gate at the end
of the wood. Beyond this the bridleway

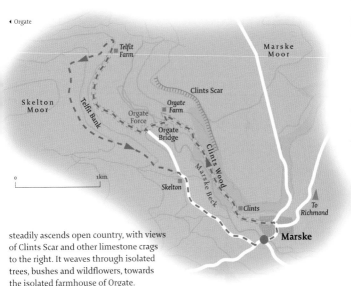

◄ Orgate

Telfit Farm

Marske Moor

Clints Scar

Orgate Farm

Skelton Moor

Telfit Bank

Orgate Force

Orgate Bridge

Clints Wood

Marske Beck

0   1km

Skelton

Clints

To Richmond

Marske

steadily ascends open country, with views of Clints Scar and other limestone crags to the right. It weaves through isolated trees, bushes and wildflowers, towards the isolated farmhouse of Orgate.

Just before the house, keep on the concrete road which veers sharply to the left and then twists downhill. Cross Marske Beck on the footbridge. The waterfall of Orgate Force lies a short way upstream, but there is no public access. At a junction with a lane, keep straight ahead along a farm road towards Telfit. This bends sharp right and then hugs the steep side of Telfit Bank, running along the edge of the broad, flat valley floor.

Keep to the left of the buildings at Telfit, the bridleway rising diagonally above the farm. Climb steeply, soon doubling back to the left. At the top of the

steep section, pass through a gateway and continue uphill on the right-hand side of a large field, going through another gate. Shortly after this, meet a path crossing the track and turn left here.

Ponder the views back over the valley of Marske Beck and across the vast heather moors to the north and west. The track now makes a long sweep around the top of Telfit Bank, running along the edge of Skelton Moor. After about 1.5km it reaches a wide-verged walled lane, dropping back into the valley. When it joins the valley road, turn right and follow this for about 1.5km to Marske Bridge.

Reeth and Grinton

Distance 4km **Time** 2 hours
Terrain riverside meadows and paths
Map OS Explorer OL30 **Access** buses from
Richmond and Keld to Reeth

Reeth stands just above the confluence of the River Swale and the Arkle Beck. Its wide green is surrounded by shops, cafés and houses and the village now thrives as a tourist destination. Its history is varied with a market charter dating back to 1695. It later became important as an industrial centre at the heart of Swaledale's lead mining bonanza. The population of Reeth once reached over 1500, twice as large as today. A short circular walk explores both Reeth and Grinton, as well as following the River Swale itself.

Go to the southwest corner of the village green (next to the National Park Centre). Walk through Anvil Square and follow the sign to the river. Go through a short alleyway and past some bungalows. Turn left and then, at a T-junction, turn right (SP Doctor's surgery). The narrow lane soon becomes a track signed for the Swing Bridge. Just before a gate, turn left and take the walled path downhill (SP Harkerside and Grinton). This soon reaches the Swale and veers right to follow the river through an area of newly planted trees to reach Reeth Swing Bridge. It's actually a suspension bridge, built in 2002 to replace the crossing built in 1920 which was destroyed by a gale in 2000.

Cross the bridge and on the far side follow the riverside path downstream (SP Grinton). The humps and hollows in the floor of the valley indicate the changing course of the Swale, and the footpath traces a route round the southern edge of this floodplain. It leads to an undulating, tree-lined

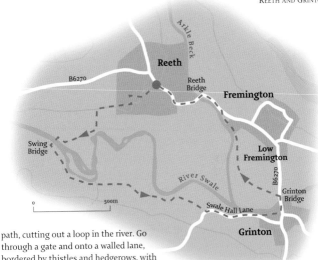

Reeth
B6270
Reeth Bridge
Fremington
Arkle Beck
Swing Bridge
Low Fremington
B6270
River Swale
Grinton Bridge
Swale Hall Lane
Grinton
0   500m

path, cutting out a loop in the river. Go through a gate and onto a walled lane, bordered by thistles and hedgerows, with views across the valley to Reeth.

As the path rejoins the riverside, it becomes a tranquil and picturesque promenade, bordered in season by meadow cranesbill, purple knapweed and harebells. Ash trees lean down to the water's edge. The path again leaves the riverbank and comes to Swale Hall Lane, just below the old buildings at Swale Hall. This was the property of Bridlington Priory until the Dissolution of the Monasteries in the 16th century. It was then the home of the Swales, a well-known local family. As you approach Grinton village, just a few metres before the 30mph sign, look out for a footpath sign on the left. Climb down the steps to the riverbank and follow the footpath at the water's edge, past the graveyard and the church.

Grinton was originally the main town of Upper Swaledale and this was the parish church for a large area. In medieval times, the dead were brought from far flung corners of the dale, along the Corpse Way, to be buried here. The ecclesiastical centre of the dale remained firmly here in Grinton and a parish church was never built in Reeth. The mining town remained firmly non-conformist territory.

Arriving at the road, turn left to cross Grinton Bridge. On the far side, go through a small gate and down some steps to follow the footpath towards Reeth. The route is surfaced and fenced as it crosses the meadows, before coming alongside Arkle Beck. On reaching the road, turn left and cross Reeth Bridge back into the village.

◄ Reeth Swing Bridge

Fremington Edge and the Arkle Beck

Distance 13km **Time** 4 hours 30
Terrain remote moorland tracks, steep
ascent and rocky descent; riverside paths
Map OS Explorer OL30 **Access** buses from
Richmond and Keld to Reeth

Reeth was the centre of Swaledale's
18th-century lead mining industry.
This walk visits many of the evocative
remains and historic sites scattered
across Fremington Edge and Marrick
Moor before returning along a riverside
route through Arkengarthdale.

From Reeth village green, walk downhill
on the main road and cross the Arkle Beck
on Reeth Bridge. On the far side, the road
turns sharply to the right. Go through a
small gate to the left on this bend and
take the footpath across a series of fields.
Climb a small bank to join a lane, then
turn left after a cottage to follow a sunken
footpath climbing to the right of the

house. In a while, rejoin the lane and
follow it all the way up Fremington Edge.
It's a steady ascent, at first through ash,
rowan and sycamore woodland, with
walls clad in moss and Herb-Robert. Later
there are good views up Arkengarthdale
and Swaledale, the two valleys divided by
the bulk of Calver Hill. The lane weaves
among the old quarries of Fremington
Edge, climbing relentlessly and later
becoming a stony track.

At the top of the escarpment, come to a
gate and a wall running along the Edge.
Go through the gate and continue on the
track towards Hurst. The scenery is now
very different with a vast vista of heather
moors stretching as far as you can see.
The track rises slightly and then descends
gradually to reach the isolated hamlet of
Hurst. Pass to the right of a reconstructed
chimney and meet a lane.

Head through a gate and turn left,
following a public bridleway sign to go

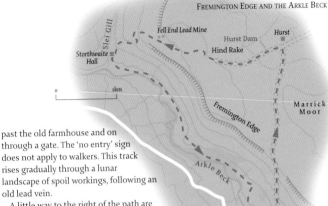

past the old farmhouse and on through a gate. The 'no entry' sign does not apply to walkers. This track rises gradually through a lunar landscape of spoil workings, following an old lead vein.

A little way to the right of the path are the remains of Hurst Dam. Follow this path for 1km, later winding up past some grouse butts before reaching the top of the moor and returning to the escarpment.

At this point, watch carefully for a bridleway post indicating where you should leave the main track and bear left to follow a lesser, rutted track. Shortly afterwards, go through a gate. Don't continue level with the wall; instead bear slightly left towards an area of hummocks and old workings. In mist a compass may be useful at this point. A narrow path leads downhill through the remains of Fell End Lead Mine. A series of cairns and small marker posts now show the way.

Ahead lies the deep trench of Slei Gill and the ravages of North Rake Hush on the other side, where lead ore has been washed out of the hillside by torrents of water. The little settlement of Booze clings to the slope opposite. As it reaches the gulf of Slei Gill, the bridleway bears left around the side of the valley and becomes a clearer track as it meanders on

through old lead mine workings. Eventually turn left through a gate, following the bridleway down a field to reach a junction next to Storthwaite Hall.

Turn left along a walled lane past a few cottages. At the end of the lane the bridleway goes through a series of meadows leading down to Arkle Beck. When the bridleway and footpath divide, bear right and keep along the water's edge all the way to Reeth. Generally, the path is clear and there are markers and signposts showing the way, so there shouldn't be too much difficulty.

The path continues through a sequence of riverside meadows near Arkle Beck to reach the road by Reeth Bridge. Cross the bridge and follow the road back to the village green.

◀ Fell End Lead Mine

Slei Gill and Booze Moor

Distance 7km **Time** 2 hours 30
Terrain riverside and moorland paths
Map OS Explorer OL30 **Access** no public
transport to the start

Arkengarthdale is one of the major
side valleys of the Swale and extends
northwest from Reeth for nearly 15km
into the wild moorland between
Yorkshire and County Durham. The
picturesque hamlet of Langthwaite is the
main settlement and is reached from the
valley road by crossing a narrow bridge
over the Arkle Beck. Lead mining has left
its mark across much of the area and here
is no exception. After a tranquil riverside
start, this walk penetrates the exploited
workings in the deep recess of Slei Gill,
then climbs grouse and heather moors to
enjoy panoramic views of the dale.

In the 19th-century heyday of lead
mining, the dale had a population of 1500
served by seven churches and nine pubs.

Now there is just one pub, the welcoming
Red Lion Inn in Langthwaite's cosy village
square, found 5km northwest of Reeth
along a minor road. From the inn, follow
the public bridleway as it wobbles
between the houses and then
accompanies the Arkle Beck downstream.
A shady promenade continues for nearly
1km until the track swings a little way
from the water's edge and climbs up to a
wooded terrace. Where the track splits,
take the left fork, following the bridleway.
After the gate the woodland gives way to
pasture, with views of the scree and scars
of Fell End Lead Mine draped down the
slope of Fremington Edge.

Where the track turns down to the right
to cross a beck, keep straight ahead,
abandoning the bridleway for a level
grassy path heading up the gill. In around
200m, where it forks, keep straight ahead
on the lower path, just above the beck.
A good trail now leads into Slei Gill with

◀ Langthwaite

the remains of lead workings all around. Further up, you pass several deep gullies and hushes, where mineral ore has been flushed out of the rocks by releasing dammed water.

As the valley closes in, the path becomes narrower and squeezes past a series of waterfalls. At some ruins and an old culvert, cross the beck and climb the far bank. Continue over a short swampy section to a grass path. Heather now dominates the view and as you climb further, aim for the shooting hut on the horizon. Just above the hut, meet a shooters' track. Turn left and follow the stony trail for over 1km, at first through the remains of the White Gang and Windegg lead veins and then above Arkengarthdale.

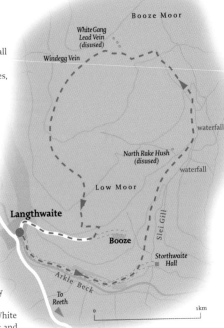

Where the main track descends and doubles back sharply to the right, keep straight ahead, bearing left onto a side track. Continue the gentle descent along the edge of Arkengarthdale. In about 700m the trail bends round to the left, just above a wall and old byre. At this point, follow the marker to bear right, off the track, following the bridleway down to a gate. Beyond the gate continue down the side of the next few enclosures near to

the wall to reach a T-junction with a bridleway. Turn left here and go down a sunken track towards the hamlet of Booze. The name refers to a settlement on a curve and is not a comment on the social aspirations of the area.

At the bottom, as you approach the houses, double back to the right and soon join the main access track from Booze. It becomes a pleasant lane, meandering down steeply to reach Langthwaite.

Gunnerside Gill

Distance 9km **Time** 3 hours
Terrain exciting rocky dale, with some
uneven paths, sometimes slippery
Map OS Explorer OL30 **Access** bus from
Richmond and Keld to Gunnerside

Gunnerside Gill drives a deep cleft
through the lead-rich moors of Swaledale
for 5km and is one of the deepest and
rockiest of the river's side dales. The
extensive remains of 19th-century lead
mining add to the drama, particularly in
the series of hushes, where dammed water
washed gravel and silt down to the dale
floor, exposing valuable minerals, while
ruined mine buildings and offices
contribute to the sense of atmospheric
devastation. The riverside path explores
the woodlands of the lower dale before
visiting the industrial relics higher up,
with a speedier return on the old mine
road offering a panorama across the valley.

Start in the centre of Gunnerside village,
by the bridge across Gunnerside Beck.
Take the path immediately to the right
(east) of the bridge (SP Gunnerside Gill).
The path soon deviates right around a
house, but then continues alongside the
beck through woodland, with the steep
sides of the gill rising up through stone
and bracken. The route is rocky and
uneven but easy enough to follow. When
you have a choice of routes, at the top of
some steps, stay on the woodland path.
It rises above the beck and may be
slippery in places. Just over 2km from
Gunnerside, as the woodland ends, cross a
small plank bridge and a couple of stiles.
Negotiate a short boggy section on the
floor of the valley before arriving at the
remains of the spoil heaps from the Sir
Francis Mine. Galena (lead ore) was
produced here by crushing the mineral
rocks extracted from the mine between

Friarfold
Moor

Blakethwaite
Smelt Mill ▫

Lownathwaite
Lead Mines
(disused)

Bunton Hush
(disused)

Gunnerside Gill

0   1km

Sir Francis
Mine

Gunnerside Beck

Gunnerside
Pasture

Gunnerside

To
Reeth

B6270

B6270

1864 and 1882. The remains of the offices and stables lie on the other side of the beck.

The route now passes just above the valley floor and then climbs diagonally through bracken, becoming a good wide path. It rises above the intake wall and continues high above the floor of the gill, eventually reaching a cairn at a junction of tracks. Keep straight on here, joining a bridleway, with a comprehensive view of the devastated remains towards the head of the gill. Bunton Hush is the immediate objective. Hushing was a technique used to expose lead ore by the force of water; a dam would be built and then breached, allowing the released water to wash away soil and gravel and reveal the minerals below. Continue on the main path through the remains of Bunton Mine. A fingerpost marks a path junction. Keep straight on here, staying on the rising path (SP Blakethwaite Dam). In another 600m there is a small cairn above a junction of valleys next to the ruins of Blakethwaite Smelt Mill.

From the cairn, a small path zigzags steeply down to the ruins and crosses the beck on a footbridge. This avoids fording Gunnerside Beck further upstream. You still have to ford the lesser watercourse of Blind Gill before taking the rising path heading south on the far bank. It climbs

gradually, but soon gains a vantage point high above the gill, with panoramic views of the extensive lead workings on the far side. In just over 1km join a track sweeping in from the right, then curving round the head of the rocky ravine of Botcher Gill. Go through the gate beyond this and continue along the old mine road for 3km to reach the lane between Gunnerside and Ivelet. Turn left and follow the lane down into Gunnerside.

Keld and Kisdon Hill

Distance 10km **Time** 4 hours
**Terrain mostly excellent tracks, with
some field paths; several hills including
a long, steep ascent up Kisdon**
**Map OS Explorer OL30 Access bus from
Richmond and Keld to Muker**

**The outward leg of this splendid circuit
of Upper Swaledale follows the river
upstream from the picturesque centre of
Muker to Keld, the highest village in the
dale. It passes the former lead workings
at Swinner Gill and continues above the
Swale Gorge and Kisdon Force waterfall.
The return route makes use of an ancient
corpse road across Kisdon.**

There is a village shop and tearoom in
the centre of Muker. Take the side road
uphill to the right (north) and pass the
public hall before curving around to some
cottages at the top of the bank. Follow
signposts for Gunnerside and Keld on a
paved path across meadows, with
traditional stone byres scattered across
the small fields on the floor of the valley.
After reaching the bank of the Swale turn

right for Gunnerside and cross the river by
Ramps Holme footbridge.

On the far side, turn left to follow the
bridleway. The wild upper reaches of
Swaledale now beckon. The river stretches
through a broad, stony floodplain,
colonised by thistles. Trees cling to the
steep sides of the dale, rising to the bleak
high pastures and moorland above. An
excellent broad stone track continues up
the dale, at first along the flat floodplain,
then climbing above the river. After 2km,
the rocky defile of Swinner Gill tumbles in
from the right. A small but powerful beck
cascades down a series of waterfalls,
arriving at the crumbling vestiges of a
smelt mill for lead ore. Cross the
footbridge and continue on the track
which now winds steadily uphill, soon
gaining a wide panorama over the valley.
Pass just below the former Crackpot Hall,
a ruined 18th-century farmhouse
abandoned in the 1950s but restored in
1999. Head for the spoil heaps ahead, the
remains of the Beldi Hill lead mines. The
track bends round to the left of the

◀ Falls of East Stonesdale

remains, passing an old byre. It continues along a delightful terrace, at the top of a vertiginous scree, diving down to the Swale's wooded gorge below. Here the river has forced a route through the rock on the northern side of Kisdon. The Swale originally followed a route to the west and south via Thwaite. Weave downhill to cross East Stonesdale Beck. Just after the footbridge, bear left to follow the Pennine Way towards Keld. Continue alongside a sequence of secluded waterfalls to reach the bottom of the Swale's wooded gorge. Cross the footbridge and climb the steps to reach a path junction. Turn right to take the level, gravelled path into Keld, arriving at the end of the road in the highest village in Swaledale.

Turn left to follow the road past the Countryside and Heritage Centre, the chapel and public toilets. Climb the hill out of the village until it comes to the 'main' road. Keep left here towards Reeth, walking alongside the road to the bottom of the hill, before bearing left along a bridleway. This is the old corpse road, climbing across Kisdon to Muker. Cross the beck before a steep climb up the flank of the hill. When the stone lane veers left, just after a house, carry straight ahead on the bridleway, now a grassy track. There's

a great sense of remoteness here, at the head of the dale, with the roof of the Pennines and the watershed just a few kilometres to the west.

As the path approaches some limestone crags and scree on the edge of the top, it veers slightly left, going towards the crown of the hill and soon arriving onto open moorland. Go through the gate and continue over the brow, heading down towards Swaledale, with a view across Muker and beyond. Curve down to the right to follow a walled green lane and continue the descent towards Muker, wandering back down to the village on a farm road.

95

Index